AF345297

Literary Recreations

LITERARY RECREATIONS;

OR

MORAL, HISTORICAL, AND RELIGIOUS,

𝕰𝖘𝖘𝖆𝖞𝖘:

BY HENRY CARD, A.M.

OF

PEMBROKE COLLEGE, OXFORD.

SECOND EDITION,

REVISED AND CONSIDERABLY ENLARGED.

LIVERPOOL:

PRINTED BY HARRIS, BROTHERS,

FOR LONGMAN, HURST, REES, ORME, AND BROWNE,

LONDON.

1811.

TO

THOMAS CHARLES CADOGAN, Esq.

WITH A

DEEP RESPECT FOR HIS VIRTUES,

This Work

IS INSCRIBED,

BY HIS MOST SINCERE,

AND MOST OBLIGED FRIEND,

THE AUTHOR.

CHAPEL HILL, MARGATE,
NOV. 1, 1810.

ADVERTISEMENT

TO THE

SECOND EDITION.

IN offering to the public a revised and enlarged impression of this work, the author conceives it would be downright affectation in him to pass over in total silence the objections that have been made to its *original title*, by some judicious and much esteemed friends: he must deem it, however, matter of high gratification, that in a work, embracing so many topics, he has not afforded them more weighty causes for objection. But, as a highly respectable Review is likewise of opinion, that the title "*might* "*be more properly exchanged, for the graver* "*one of Dissertations, moral, historical, and re-* "*ligious*[*]," he is induced to think, that the al-

---

[*] Vide the British Critic, for the month of January, 1810.

teration now made, in that respect, will be more likely to obtain their approbation.

The author likewise, cannot omit this opportunity of noticing another point, upon which some little explanation is due to his readers. In his Essay " *On the rapid growth of Methodism,*" he is supposed to have involved, under the suspicious name of methodists, all those who are in any degree conspicuous for their piety and holiness of character, gravity of manners, and reverential study of the sacred records. To this, he must beg leave to answer, that he has been greatly misunderstood, and that nothing was more remote from his intention. He meant only to designate by that name, *those self-constituted teachers of religion,* and their followers ;—a set of fanatics, who fancying themselves exalted above the common condition of the faithful, have assumed the vain but impious task, of undermining those foundations upon which the fabric of our establishment is reared ;—men who are obviously as much the bane of literature as of religion; since

the advancement of literature is as favourable
to true piety, as it is fatal to canting and superstition. If then, he has not spoken of them
in a tone of uniform calmness, or of guarded
caution, when, to borrow an expression of
Cicero, *est inter nos non de terminis, sed de tota
possessione contentio,*—if he has not always observed a measured language in exposing their
hypocrisy and fanaticism, from which have
flowed mischiefs innumerable upon all those
who are within the sphere of their influence;
—he will not surely be confounded among
those bigots, who hold, that orthodoxy atones
for all vices, and that heresy extinguishes all
virtues.

To the present edition, a copious Index is
annexed, which will be found at the end of the
volume.

CONTENTS.

LITERARY

RECREATIONS.

═══════

ESSAY I.

ON THE ORIGIN OF EULOGIES.

THE love of praise is so generally prevalent, that without fear of contradiction, it may be regarded as a common principle, inherent in human nature, because it seems inseparable from self-love. This passion, has rendered some men as conspicuous for their crimes, as it has others, for their virtues. It has produced princes and generals, who have done the work of demons, in order to obtain the name of heroes; and it has also given birth to the systems of the legislator, and to the eloquence of the orator. Fools and flatterers have not been wanting to confound those two classes of men. But their panegyrics may be said to resemble the statues erected by the Romans to their emperors; most of which were broken to pieces, when the object of them ceased to exist.

Death, does, indeed, make as much havoc with the reputation of the former class, as they did with their swords, when living, among their fellow creatures. Fear and interest, being no longer constrained to pour forth their eulogies, their memories are consigned at once to the vengeance of posterity. How differently does death operate upon the characters of the benefactors of mankind? The voice of envy is then heard no more against them; and immortality commences*. That such is the immutable distinction established by the fiat of after-ages, between these classes of men, cannot escape the observation of those, who have been accustomed to survey the history of the world with an attentive eye.

The origin of eulogies, prior, as they unquestionably were, to civil institutions, may yet form the subject of an entertaining and instructive essay; for the desire of knowing what has happened in ages, when the use of arts and letters was unknown, can never be coupled with absurdity, so long as it is attended with the beneficial consequence of enabling us to appreciate more fully the blessings of civilization.

To the first hymns addressed to the Deity, we may

* Urit enim fulgore suo qui prægravat artes,
   Infra se positas; extinctus amabitur idem.—*Horace, Epist. I. Lib. ii.*

safely ascribe the origin of eulogies. These hymns were inspired by admiration and gratitude. Man, in his primæval state, on contemplating the magnificent canopy of Heaven, the boundless immensity of the waters, the deep gloom of the forests, the endless variety and richness of the fields, and the innumerable multitude of beings, destined to ornament the globe which he inhabited, must have been impressed with the feelings of admiration and delight. To these, another sentiment would necessarily succeed. When the transports of wonder had subsided at this august spectacle, he could not fail to discover that he was not the author of it, but that it was the work of an all-wise, all-powerful, and all-benevolent Being. Possessed of this religious idea, he must then have joined his voice to that of nature, and sung forth, with the most lively sensations of gratitude, the praises of Him, who enabled him to perceive, and feel, the incomparable beauty of the universe.

The first hymn chanted in this solitude of the world, observes an elegant and profound writer*, was a great epoch for the human race. Soon after that event, parents, we may suppose, assembled their children in the fields, to offer up the same homage. Then did

* See the beautiful " Essai sur les Eloges," by M. Thomas.—*Tom. I. p. 2.*

the aged sire, holding a blade of corn in one hand, and, with the other, pointing to the earth, sea, and skies, instruct his family to sound the praises of the God who nourished them.

> These are thy glorious works, Parent of good,
> Almighty! thine this universal frame,
> Thus wondrous fair; thyself how wondrous, then!
> Unspeakable; who sit'st above the heav'ns,
> To us invisible, or dimly seen,
> In these thy lowest works; yet these declare
> Thy goodness beyond thought, and power divine.
>
> *Paradise Lost, Book* v.

In this reign of nature, thanksgivings were likewise repeated at the rising and setting of the sun, the renewal of the year, the commencement of a season, and the appearance of a new moon. In ages more advanced into a state of regular policy, we discover the constant practice of addressing the gods upon all occasions of happiness, or misery. When battles were fought, and won, or when pestilence and famine visited them, the people equally crowded the temple, to celebrate the praises of the deities they adored.

In those hymns, which were sung in that country where Homer poured forth his immortal lines, and Orpheus instituted his mysteries, and which are still left entire to us, it is easy to discover passages of great sublimity, disfigured as they are by the idle tales of superstition. The hymns attributed to Homer, partake of the grandeur and beauty of his poetry; yet may rather be regarded as monuments of ancient mythology, than of religious eulogies. Tradition has handed down to us, the unrivalled fame which Pindar obtained for his hymns to Jupiter, his pæans to Apollo, and his lofty dithyrambics* to Bacchus. But the hand of time has not spared one of those performances; all that can now be safely affirmed of them is, that they were consecrated to the Delphian Apollo, whose oracles equally laid under contribution, the credulity of the people, and the ambition of kings. It may, however, be reasonably doubted, whether even the muse of Pindar could have soared to an higher pitch of sublimity, than is to be found in the following hymn of Cleanthes. Animated by his divine subject, he thus breaks forth in strains worthy, in every respect, of the father of the Stoics†.

* Laurea donandus Apollinari,
   Seu per audaces nova dithyrambos
   Verba devolvit, numerisque fertur,
      Lege solutis;
   Seu Deos, regesque canit, Deorum,
      Sanguinem.   *Horace, Lib. iv. Ode 2.*

† The appellation given him by Cicero, although he was the disciple and successor of Zeno, the founder of the Portico.

" O thou, who, under several names art adored, but whose power is entire and infinite, O Jupiter, first of immortals, sovereign of nature, governor of all, and supreme legislator of all things, accept my suppliant prayer, for to man is given the right to invoke thee. Whatever lives and moves on this earth, drew its being from thee; we are a faint similitude of thy divinity. I will address, then, my hymns to thee, and never will I cease to praise thy wondrous power. That universe, suspended over our heads, and which seems to roll around the earth, obeys thee; it moves along, and silently submits to thy mandate. The thunder, minister of thy laws, rests under thy invincible hands, flaming, gifted with an immortal life, it strikes, and all nature is terrified. Thou directest the universal spirit, which animates all things, and lives in all beings. Such, O Almighty King, is thy unbounded sway! In heaven, on earth, or in the floods below, there is nought performed, or produced, without thee, except the evil, which springs from the heart of the wicked*.

* Ουδε τι γιγνεται εργον επι χθονι σου διχα, δαιμον,

Ουτε κατ' αιθεριον θειον πολον, ουτ'ιν ποντω

Πλην οποσα ρεζουσι κακοι σφιτερησιν ανοιαις.——*Lines* 15—17.

How similar is this sentiment to that expression of the Apostle St. James; " Let no man say, when he is tempted, I am tempted of God, for God cannot be tempted with evil, neither tempteth he any man."

Epist. Chap. i. 13.

By thee, confusion is changed into order: by thee, the warring elements are united. By an happy agreement, thou so blendest good with evil, as to produce a general and eternal harmony in all things. But man, wicked man, alone, breaks this great harmony of the world. Wretched being, who seeks after good, and yet perceives not the universal law which points out the way to render him at once good and happy! He abandons the pursuit of virtue and justice, and roves where each passion moves him. Sordid wealth, fame, and sensual pleasures, become, by turns, the objects of his pursuit. O God, from whom all gifts descend, who sittest in thick darkness*, thunder-ruling Lord, dispel this ignorance from the mind of man; deign to enlighten his soul; draw it to that eternal reason which serves as thy guide, and support, in the government of the world! So that, honoured with a portion of this light, we may, in our turn, be able to honour thee, by celebrating thy great works unceasingly, in a hymn. This is the proper duty of man. For, surely, nothing can be more delightful to the inhabitants of the earth, or the skies,

* Αλλα Ζι παιδωρι, κιλαινιφις, αρχικιραυνι.—*Line* 32. " He made darkness his secret place; his pavilion round about him were dark waters, and thick clouds of the skies."—*Psalm xviii. v.* 11. The hymn of Cleanthes is preserved by Stobæus.

Edit. Heeren. Tom. I. p. 30, 35.

than to celebrate that divine reason which presides over nature."

Among the Roman poets, Ovid addressed a hymn to Bacchus, Virgil one to Hercules, and Horace has given us several, which discover that grace and harmony of versification, of which he was confessedly so great a master. But the above ode of Cleanthes is entitled to a decided preference over them all, not only from the superior sublimity of thought, but from the inimitable grandeur of expression*.

Eulogies were not, however, long confined to the Deity, but descended soon to man. They began in truth, but have ended in adulation. They celebrated benefits, before they flattered power, and honoured crimes. The reason of this proceeding is obvious. In rude ages, man stood fierce, and independent. In the equality of rights, which then existed, to receive praise, was to merit it. The chief, or rather the sole, ground of distinction, being personal qualities, he who performed the most useful services, was sure to be the most admired and respected.

* It may not be amiss here to observe, that our reason for making no mention of the sacred hymns and songs addressed by the Hebrews to the Deity, arises from respect, and the persuasion, that it would be highly improper to pass any criticism upon performances which breathe so divine a spirit of eloquence.

The discovery of fire, the application of this element to the uses of life, the art of forging metals, and the rude design of a plough, were doubtless the first titles for the panegyrics of nations. The meanest professions were then the noblest. After these discoverers of materials adapted to the purposes of life had received their due praises, the next persons to whom, we may suppose, the palm of distinction and honor was assigned, were those who voluntarily encountered lions and tigers, and other destructive animals, to ensure the safety and preservation of their fellow creatures. The legislator may be conjectured to have been the last, in this infant state of society, who was exalted to a place among the benefactors of mankind*.

The existence, indeed, of eulogies, among the earliest ages of the world, can be readily traced by every writer, who has applied himself to the study of general history. The Chinese, Phœnicians, and Arabians, celebrated in songs the great exploits of their heroes. Greece could not be recognised as the country of Homer and Plato, when she adopted or created this usage.

* The Gods of Greece and Rome, as well as of other nations, had been men, inventors of useful arts, victorious rulers, and wise legislators, who had been deified after their deaths.

See Cicero de Naturâ Deorum, Lib. i. Diodorus Siculus, Lib. iii. Cæsar de Bel. Gal. Lib. vi. 17.

The same custom was practised among the Romans, when the blood of a horse, the husk of a bean, the ashes of the bowels of a calf killed in the belly of its mother, and burnt on the altar of Vesta, were deemed sufficient to purify their nation*.

In short, the same institution prevailed for several centuries among the Celtic people. The Druids were the philosophers and priests of the nation; the Bards were the panegyrists of heroes†. Their station was the centre of the army; and the warrior, who fell, covered with a hundred wounds, turned his dying eyes towards the poet, who was to raise him to a state of immortality. These songs or eulogies constituted the chief glory of that nation. The memory of those songs passed to succeeding generations. They served as the prelude to battles; they animated the warrior; they consoled the aged. The hero, who could no longer wield the javelin, seated himself under an oak, and listened with delight to the bard, who rehearsed the glorious deeds of his youth; while his sons, who surrounded him, leaned upon their lances, and sighed to think how distant might be the period before they should equal his renown.

* See Ovid, Fasti. *Lib. iv.*

† See Henry's History of Great Britain, *vol. i. p.* 141, 145, 153.

The enthusiasm of valor, which these panegyrics tended to call forth among the people, may be more easily
conceived than described. Such, indeed, were the
effects of those military songs, that we may almost be
justified in comparing them to the Roman triumphs,
which, by exhibiting symbols of the cities, rivers, and
mountains, the general had visited in the course of his
victorious career, exposed to the eyes of the citizens
the magnitude of his conquests; and never failed to
excite in them sentiments the most conducive to the
permanent glory of their country. By means of these
songs, Germany, Gaul, and England, maintained so
long a struggle against the Roman power; and they imparted to the north of Scotland a sentiment of liberty
and independence, which is not even yet entirely extinguished. Before Edward the First could subdue
the Welsh, he was obliged to have recourse to the
cruel expedient of massacring their bards. But, though
he put them to the sword, he could not destroy those
songs which perpetuated, in their mountains, a contempt of death, and an abhorrence of slavery.

The Germans, like the Scots and Britons, had their
bards, who, in the field of battle, and the feast of
victory, animated their auditors to imitate the illustrious
exploits of their forefathers. Several of their songs

existed in the time of Charlemagne, who ordered them to be translated into verse, in the language of the ancient *Romantz**. These monuments were preserved, as long as this great prince lived; but they were swept away in the deluge of barbarism, which followed his death. An historian, however, who wrote in the commencement of the sixteenth century, pretends to quote those ancient songs which he is said to have discovered in some convent of Germany; but whoever has examined the general nature of the events recorded in his work, will not be inclined, perhaps, to give implicit belief to this assertion+.

If we ascend from Germany towards the north, among the Scandinavians, we shall find the same usage existing. The people, who reduced the mistress of the world, had a subject to celebrate, powerfully adapted to kindle enthusiasm and valour in their ferocious breasts. The Scaldi sung the glories of their heroes; and, it is said, that the Runic characters are still to be traced on the rocks of the north. The Danes, who, under the famous name of Normans, spread devastation

---

* See remarks upon the origin of that species of writing, in " The reign of Charlemagne, considered chiefly with reference to religion, laws, literature, and manners."—*Page* 201, *&c.*

+ See the Chronicon of Albert Krantzius.

over the largest and finest part of Europe, never failed
to be accompanied, on their piratical expeditions, by
a number of Scaldi, or poets, selected for the express
purpose of recording their exploits.

The same usage prevailed in America. In Mexico,
Peru, Brazil, and Canada, poets have arisen to celebrate different sorts of great men. Thus, by a very
natural order of things, it seems, that public interest
laid the foundation of eulogies. Each nation considered that as most praise-worthy, which most administered to its wants and pleasures. Piracy was,
therefore, the theme of universal applause among the
Scandinavians, plunder among the Huns, fanaticism
among the Arabs, the benevolent and useful virtues
among civilized people, hunting and fishing among
savages, and navigation among the inhabitants of islands.

Having now briefly surveyed the origin of eulogies,
of almost every nation of the earth, it will not be
widely deviating from the subject of this essay, to close
it with paying a tribute of admiration to that practice,
observed for so many centuries in Egypt, preparatory
to the interment of her people and chief magistrates;
and, which no nation, ancient or modern, has ever
dared to imitate, although it was so pregnant with real

good and greatness. We are informed*, by that eminent Greek historian, Diodorus Siculus, that a tribunal was erected among the Egyptians, where subjects, and princes themselves, were judged, and condemned or acquitted, after their deaths; where the memories of the wicked citizen and courtier, and profligate tyrant, who had escaped the punishment due to their numerous crimes, were delivered up to eternal infamy; and where the fathers of their people, and all, whose labours had tended to promote the public good, and private happiness, received those panegyrics and honours which

* *Lib. i. p.* 83, 84, 103. The manner of proceeding was as follows:—On the day appointed for the royal funeral, a public audience was assembled, and accusations were received against the deceased monarch. The priests then began the solemnity, with pronouncing his panegyric, and celebrating his good actions. If the monarch had really reigned well, the innumerable multitudes who attended, answered the priests with loud acclamations; but a general murmur ensued, if he had reigned ill; and some kings have been even deprived of burial by the decision of the people. Now this custom of judging their kings after death may be traced up to the earliest ages of the Egyptian monarchy. (See Diodorus Siculus, *Lib. i. p.* 84.) And it is worthy of remark, that it appeared to the Israelites so wise a practice, that they in part adopted it. We see in Scripture, that the kings who reigned ill were not buried in the sepulchre of their fathers. (See Chronicles, *cap. xxi, v.* 19, 20; *cap. xxiv. v.* 25; *cap. xxviii. v.* 27. II. Kings, *c. xxi. v.* 26.) Josephus also informs us, that this custom was observed in the time of the Asmonæan princes.—See Antiquities, *Lib. xiii. cap. xxiii.*

had been withheld from them when living*. What
an edifying and imposing situation! How powerfully
calculated to interest the best affections of the mind;
and how worthy of that country, which was the cradle
of arts, sciences, and mysteries†, the school of Orpheus
and Homer, Pythagoras and Plato, Solon and Lycurgus.
To such an institution, which so well deserves to live
in the voice and memory of men, we may, with the
strictest propriety, apply those emphatic words of the
Roman Historian, " *Præcipuum munus annalium reor, ne
virtutes sileantur; utque pravis dictis factisque ex poste-
ritate et infamiâ metus sit‡.*"

* Although some critics refuse their assent to the general opinion of
the Sixth Book of the Æneid being the most perfect of the whole, in point
of sublime invention, beauty of imagery, majesty of sentiment, and
harmony of versification; assuredly they will not deny, that, from
the beginning to the end, we may discover the strokes of a master.
Those passages, especially, interest our moral feelings, where, under
the just empire of Minos, the poet displays his eloquence, in describing
the punishments of wickedness, the happiness of the patriot who died
for his country, and the misery of the tyrant who oppressed it.

† " The Egyptians, (says the very learned President de Goguet, in his
Origin of Laws, Arts, &c. *vol. I. b.* 1. *art. iv.)* of all nations, are most
worthy of our attention. We are particularly interested in their history.
From them, by an uninterrupted chain, all the most polite, and best
constituted nations of Europe, have received the first principles of their
laws, arts, and sciences. The Egyptians instructed and enlightened
the Greeks; the Greeks performed the same beneficent office to the
Romans." &c.

‡ Tacitus, *Lib. iii. cap. lxv.*

ESSAY II.

ON SOME PARTICULAR INJUNCTIONS AND ACTIONS IN THE NEW TESTAMENT.

IT is the opinion of many good Christians, that, as the clergy are allowed so short a time in every year to instruct their fellow-creatures from the pulpit, their discourses ought, therefore, to be chiefly or solely employed upon practical subjects;—in shewing what our religion prohibits, and what it enjoins us to do, in this world, in order that we may be received to a happy immortality, in that which is to come. Yet those who may entirely subscribe to this opinion, will not, however, consider it as an impertinent interference with the concerns of the clerical profession, if we devote an essay to the interpretation of some particular injunctions and actions of our Lord; which, at the first glance, have even staggered the minds of the truly pious, and have excited doubts altogether of the divine authority of the Christian dispensation, in many thousands, whom ignorance or inattention has led to obtain but a scanty and imperfect knowledge of it. To learned men, the passages we shall select for explanation, will, doubtless, seem to be of little difficulty, and, perhaps, of no very high importance. But as this volume will, it is to be hoped, fall into the hands of others, less intimately conversant with such studies, we may be allowed, without the imputation of vanity, to think, that it may be in our power satisfactorily to answer some objections of those, who have not been accustomed to make religion alone their rule of life.

Upon the following passages, then, we shall venture to make a few comments.

——————

" So the devils besought him, saying, If thou cast us out, suffer us to go away into the herd of swine. And he said unto them, Go."—Matt. viii. 31, 32.

THE enemies of the Christian faith, with a malignant and illiberal exultation, have maintained the destruction of the herd of swine to be one of those miracles wrought by our Saviour, which, so far from advancing any moral purpose, tended to produce the most evil and mischievous consequences. And, in support of this assertion, they have brought forward every specious argument, which their sophistry could supply. But those who have pursued their enquiries respecting the miracles of our blessed Lord with more candour and impartiality, and, we will venture to add, with more erudition, can as clearly perceive the laws of justice*, and the obligations of morality, to be strictly regarded, in his sending the devils into a herd of swine, as in any other miracle which he performed, to confirm his claims to a divine commission. In their well-meaning zeal to vindicate Jesus from even being supposed as the author of the mischief here done, some divines have strongly contended, that our Saviour did not command, but only suffered, the devils, at their own request, to take possession of the swine. But the expression, Go, implies, in our opinion, something more than a bare permission; and, for giving this command, we are inclined to think these, among many other reasons, may be satisfactorily alledged.

Without entering into a discussion respecting the extent of power which evil spirits had, to influence the minds of men, during the age in which our Saviour+

---

* See, in Mr. Farmer's Essay on the Demoniacs of the New Testament, p. 294, 307, a long and able vindication of this transaction.

+ We could easily quote many expressions of the Apostles, to prove the mighty influence which the Devil, " the God of this world," as St. Paul styles him, 2 *Corinthians* iv. 4, possessed in the affairs of men. But it will be sufficient to shew his power in that respect, if we only call to remembrance the injunctions which our Lord gave to his disciples, to supplicate God to deliver them, ἀπο τυ πονηρυ, from the evil one.

appeared upon earth, it is well known, that the Jews ascribed his power of casting out devils, to Beelzebub, the prince of devils. To satisfy, then, the most suspicious, that his controul over the possessed was derived only from the divine will, he sent the devils, which he had ejected out of a poor man, into a herd of swine; and, by that act, made it equally obvious to the learned and ignorant, that, whatever compact might exist between him and the demoniacs, he could have none with the swine. Our Lord might, also, intend to shew, by this miracle, the great malice and power of the devils, and the multitude of them that possessed the one or two persons; since, on that expulsion, they were sufficient to actuate the bodies of a herd of swine, which St. Mark affirms to have consisted of no smaller number than two thousand. By a miracle like this, addressed so completely to the testimony of the senses, the most prejudiced must likewise have been sensible of the great deliverance given to those two tormented persons.

It is the opinion of Grotius*, that he wrought this miracle to convince the Greeks, who lived in Gadara, and kept the herd of swine, that the laws of the Jews were too sacred to be ridiculed with impunity by

---

* See Grotii Opera, *Tom. II. Annot. ad Matthæum, p.* 99.

them, as they were, upon account of the prohibition they contained to eat swine's flesh. How far this opinion is entitled to general reception, we shall not presume to determine; but those who may be disposed to cavil at it, will surely admit, that the destruction of the herd of swine was a just punishment upon those to whom the beasts belonged, since, by their soliciting Jesus, immediately afterwards to depart from their coasts, it is very evident, that they preferred their swine before their souls. Yet, either of the foregoing explanations, we should hope, is quite adequate to refute any objections to this miracle, on the score of its unsuitableness to any good purpose; and of its being repugnant to every principle of humanity and justice.

" Wherefore I say unto you, all manner of sin and blasphemy shall be forgiven unto men; but the blasphemy against the Holy Ghost shall not be forgiven unto men. And whosoever speaketh a word against the Son of man, it shall be forgiven him; but whosoever speaketh against the Holy Ghost, it shall not be forgiven him, neither in this world, neither in the world to come."—Matthew xii. 31, 32.

ACCORDING to their peculiar tenets, have divines

interpreted the meaning of that sin, which is emphatically styled *the sin against the Holy Ghost*. But, as their learning, like their intentions, is very different, we shall avoid much useless discussion, by briefly collecting the sentiments of the most sagacious and orthodox theologians upon this disputed point. When the three evangelists, Matthew, Mark, and Luke, so explicitly concur in representing the sin of blasphemy against the Holy Ghost, as irremissible, " οὔτε ἐν τούτω τω αἰωνι, οὔτε ἐν τω μελλοντι," it is surprising to us that so skilful a commentator as Grotius should attempt to soften the severity of this sentence, by saying, that what is absolutely spoken by our Lord, must be understood comparatively, and only implies the extreme difficulty, though not the absolute impossibility, of obtaining the pardon of this sin.

It may be observed, that, at the time that Jesus declares all hope of forgiveness is excluded from him who vilifies and blasphemes the Holy Ghost, yet a free pardon is assured to him who speaketh against the Son of man; that is, who shall style him a wine-bibber, a glutton, an impostor, and shall impute his miracles to the agency of an infernal spirit*. Now it is evident,

---

* His threatening, however, in one instance, is as strong as this in the case of blasphemy against the Holy Ghost : " Whoever shall deny me

that this heinous offence could not be committed during the actual ministry of Christ, because the Holy Ghost was not to be sent till after his glorious resurrection, and ascension into Heaven. When the descent of the Holy Ghost communicated to the disciples of our Lord the same stupendous powers he had possessed, to revile that extraordinary gift became, therefore, a sin of the most unpardonable nature, because this was the completion of the evidence of his divine mission and character. Thus it appears, that the sin against the Holy Ghost lay in totally resisting and finally rejecting the Gospel, as preached by the Apostles, who supported and established their commission " by signs and wonders, and divers miracles of the Holy Ghost." For those who had witnessed, then, their nature, greatness, and number, still to persist in denying Christ

before men," says Jesus, " him will I also deny before my Father." *Matthew, chap. x. v.* 33. And yet, when Peter, says Bishop Pearce, shortly afterwards denied him before men, three times, joining oaths and curses with his denials, nevertheless upon his repenting, and weeping bitterly, he was not only forgiven, but continued in his apostleship. Again, when Jesus was upon the Cross, some of the rulers derided him, saying, " he saved others, let him save himself if he be Christ the chosen of God," *Luke xxiii. v.* 35; by which words, it appears that they acknowledged Jesus to have wrought miracles, and yet rejected them, denying that he wrought them by the holy spirit of God : and yet Jesus prayed to his Father that they might be forgiven. *Luke, chap. xxiii. v.*34.

to be the Messiah, was a sin in them obviously distinct from all their other sins. Because, after those last infallible and decisive tests of divine interposition, it evinced a most incurable wickedness and perverseness of mind, a most unconquerable and impious aversion, to refuse " being brought to faith in Christ."

————

" *But I say unto you, that every idle word that men shall speak, they shall give account thereof in the day of judgment.*"—*Matthew xii.* 36.

By straining the sense of this declaration of Jesus, commentators lose all sight of those qualities of compassion and love for the welfare of mankind, which so eminently distinguished his doctrines. " My yoke* is easy, and my burthen is light," is the benevolent and consoling assurance of our Divine Master. Now, to interpret literally the above declaration, must produce no other effect than that of exciting horror and disgust towards the Christian religion, in the minds of the dissolute, but enlightened; and of in-

* The close similarity between this expression and the following of Plato's, is worthy of notice :—Μετρια η Θεω δυλεια; αμετρος δε η τοις ανθρωποις.—*Epist. viii.*

fusing scruples even among those who are the least in danger of imbibing the poison of infidelity. From the manner, indeed, in which some have expounded this declaration, we might even be led to infer, that it is sinful to talk of news, rain, weather, or any of those indifferent matters, which cannot be said to do either harm or good. To such trifles, this awful menace of our Lord was certainly not intended to apply.

The proper explanation of the subject we take to be this:—That men should give an account, at the day of judgment, of all the wicked and impious words which they have spoken; and that the Pharisees especially should be answerable to God for the blasphemies which they uttered against his miracles. There is a passage of Plato, in his Treatise de Fato, where he observes, " Grievous is the damage of light and frivolous words." Now, by κωφων, και κενων λογων, the philosopher evidently means words spoken against parents, or the defamation of persons to whom a due reverence ought to be paid. The παν ρημα αργον can admit, then, of no other meaning, than wicked, impious, scandalous, or false*,

* Puto autem non eum sermonem hic notari qui quoque modo sit inutilis, sed eum qui veri solidatate careat. Grotius Annot. on *Matt.* p. 132. See likewise Archbishop Newcombe's Observations on our Lord's conduct, *p.* 41.

words. Upon the same ground that we object to the literal interpretation of the above passage, we must, likewise, enter our protest against those who consider that the word *fool*, in the following sentence, *is to* be received according to the modern acceptation of that word :—" But whosoever shall say, unto his brother, *thou fool!* shall be in danger of hell fire." *Matthew v. 22.*—Since the word *fool*, here, plainly signifies a profane and wicked person, as it is shewn in the Psalms: " The fool has said in his heart, there is no God." —" Arise, O God, maintain thine own cause; remember how the foolish man blasphemeth thee daily."

" For as Jonas was three days and three nights in the whale's belly, so shall the Son of man be three days and three nights in the heart of the earth."—Matthew xii. 40.

T H E historical, as well as the moral part of the New Testament, has been alike exposed to the impotent attacks of the flagitious. But, surely, those who raise objections against the truth of these words, must be ignorant that the Jews used the phrase, 'three days and three nights,' to denote what we understand by three days. " I will cause it to rain upon the earth forty days and forty nights." *Genesis vii. 4.*—" That Egyptian did eat no bread, nor drink water, three days and three nights." *I. Samuel, xxx.* 12.—" Moses was in the Mount forty days and forty nights." *Exodus xxiv.* 18. Instead, then, of saying three days and three nights, let us simply say three days, and we think there will be no more seeming defectiveness of the fact of Christ being three days, Friday, Saturday, and Sunday, in the heart of the earth. We are not, however, to be understood as saying, that he was in the grave the whole of either Friday or Sunday. But Grotius* and Lightfoot+ tell us, that it was a received rule among the Jews, that part of the day was put for the whole; so that, according to their computation, he might be truly said to have been in the grave three days and three nights‡.

" The Son of man goeth, as it is written of him, but wo to that man by whom the Son of man is betrayed! it had been good for that man, if he had not been born."—Matthew xxvi. 24.

---

* Annot. in Matth. *p.* 133.

+ See his Exercit. upon St. Matthew, *vol. II. p.* 191, 192.

‡ See likewise some learned and ingenious illustrations upon this subject, in Gilbert Wakefield's Commentaries on St. Matthew, *p.* 181, 182.

F εw passages in the Gospel have produced a more infinite variety of opinions, than this. Some have thought it incumbent upon them to believe, that Judas was created for no other purpose but to betray the Son of God; or, in other words, that it was absolutely decreed, by the will of our Heavenly Father, that he should be as one of those vessels that were made to wrath, before the foundations of the world were laid. But they who refuse their assent to this doctrine of absolute election and reprobation, have, nevertheless, not dissembled the difficulty of reconciling this prediction of our Lord, with the common notions of divine mercy and justice. It appears to us, that we should entertain a very erroneous notion of the divine œconomy, in supposing that an antecedent necessity was imposed upon Judas, of betraying Christ, in consequence of his having foretold that event. For we cannot listen with patience to the opinion, that a Being, as wise and benevolent as he is omnipotent, should arbitrarily select one portion of the human race for eternal happiness, and consign the other to eternal misery.

To reconcile, then, the above declaration with the great fundamental doctrine of Scripture, that the Son of man descended from Heaven to redeem all mankind, we must deny, entirely, all partial providence in God, and believe, that he equally enabled Judas as any other man born in the world, to work out his salvation: but that, by his prescience, he foresaw that he would not be obedient to his laws. Upon no account, therefore, are we to conclude, that, because Judas betrayed his Master, he had less free will than any other individual of the human race. Neither are we to view the appointment of Judas to the apostleship as incompatible with that pre-eminent wisdom which characterised all the actions of our blessed Lord. Since, long before any intention was manifested by Judas to betray him, Jesus fully exposed his real character to the rest of his disciples, in these words: " Have I not chosen you twelve, and one of you is a devil ?" *John vi.* 70. That is, one whose mind is actuated by the most base and inordinate passions.

It has been also absurdly urged by the adversaries of our holy faith, that Judas was induced to betray his Master, in consequence of having discovered that he was an impostor. Or else, say they, the consideration of his power and knowledge, as the Son of God, would have terrified him from doing it. But this frivolous objection is at once refuted, by the contrition which he afterwards expressed to the chief priests and elders. " I have sinned," was his confession to them, " in betraying innocent blood." The true motive which instigated Judas to that act of perfidy, we take to be the following:—The Jewish nation, it is well known, expected to, see, in the person of their promised deliverer, a powerful king, who should liberate them from the galling yoke of the Romans; and this opinion was not confined to the rulers of the Jews, but was as readily embraced by the disciples of our Lord. So rooted was this belief among them, that we even see, not all the repeated avowals of Jesus to the contrary, could erase it from their minds. To the impatience of Judas to participate in the temporal honors and emoluments of his Master's kingdom, we must solely ascribe his subsequent perfidious conduct. So far, indeed, does he seem to have been carried away by the popular prepossessions respecting the character and office of the Messiah, that he did not doubt, upon his delivering Jesus into the hands of the Sanhedrim, that he would immediately assume the ensigns of temporal dominion, and reward his adherents with an abundance of riches; the expectation of which had first led Judas to become a disciple, for he was of a disposition so covetous, we find, as to steal money out of the common bag. The disappointment, then, of obtaining an object, which lay so near his heart, together with the remorse which he really felt at bringing his Master to an ignominious death, concurred, we may also suppose, in urging him to put an end to his own existence.

———

" And about the ninth hour Jesus cried with a loud voice, saying, Eli, Eli, lama sabacthani! that is to say, My God, my God, why hast thou forsaken me !"—Matthew xxvii. 46.

VARIOUS solutions have been given oft his tragic exclamation. We shall select those which appear to us most entitled to notice, and leave our readers to draw their own conclusions. It has pleased the enemies of Christianity to insinuate, that the divine founder of it, by the despondency which he shewed in the garden of Gethsemane, on the approach of his trial and death, and the words which he uttered upon the cross, evinced a want of manly fortitude, little calculated to support the truth of those doctrines, which he preached. In reply to these invidious remarks, many learned men contend, that it was not the fear of crucifixion, which so far overcame Jesus, as to throw him into an agony and bloody sweat, but his distress in the garden proceeded from the lively sense which he, at that time, had of the miseries of mankind, produced by sin; and that when he cried out, " My God, My God, why hast thou forsaken me!*" his anguish arose from the inconceivable pains which were inflicted on him by the hand of God, on his making his soul an offering for sin. Others, also, labour to prove, that the perplexity is occasioned by our indistinct notion of the *hypostatic union*, or else we should have perceived that the divine was, at that moment, so much lost or absorbed in his human nature, as to make him feel a withdrawing of those comforts, which hitherto had always filled his soul, although it is extremely difficult for us to imagine in what that agony consisted.

But, perhaps, the evangelists themselves will afford us a more clear conception of this subject, for in many instances we shall find that they are our best commentators. From them we learn, that the salvation of mankind was the momentous end for which Jesus came into the world; or, according to the scriptural phrase, " to give his life as a ransom for many." Upon this account, therefore, his sorrows, observes a writer of equal piety and judgment, " were such as no other person in this life ever felt. They arose from causes

* These words, says the learned Bishop Pearce, in his commentary on the Evangelists, *p.* 199, most probably were not uttered by way of complaint, but by way of pointing out the *xxii. Psalm*, which begins, with these words, as prophetical of Jesus the speaker.

altogether singular, and from circumstances peculiar to himself. Being of this sort, they were no greater than the cause merited, and the expressions by which he uttered them, are no argument of his pusillanimity or weakness. They were suitable to his feelings, and expressed them as far as it was possible to make them known: for it was agreeable to the counsels of God, and for the benefit of men, that the sorrows which the Son of God felt in that hour, should be laid open to the view of the world*."

"*And in the morning, as they passed by, they saw the fig-tree dried up from the roots. And Peter, calling to re-membrance, said, Master, behold the fig-tree which thou cursedst is withered away.*"—*Mark xi.* 20, 21.

THE cursing of the fig-tree, like the destruction of the herd of swine, has been represented, by the opponents of revealed religion, as conveying no moral lesson, and in every respect as unbecoming the character of the divine teacher of mankind. In the first place, we must observe, to curse the land or trees signifies in the Hebrew language, simply to make or pronounce them un-fruitful, as may be satisfactorily shewn in the following

* See the Truth of the Gospel History, by Macknight, *Book I. chap. iv.*

passage: "But which beareth thorns and briars is rejected, and is nigh unto cursing, whose end is to be
burned." *Hebrews* vi. 8.—The supposition, then, of
those persons, that Jesus, in cursing the tree, uttered
execrations against it, is as ill-founded as it is impious.
But his motive for cursing the tree*, that is, pronouncing it unfruitful†, was to instruct the spectators
of this miracle, that the Jews, a mere professing people, and who were just like that leaf-tree, without
fruit, were to expect speedy destruction from him, if
they persisted in their unfruitfulness‡.

This short elucidation I prefer to that of Whitby
and other commentators.

---

* The fig-tree, observes Dr. Jortin, in his admirable Remarks on
Ecclesiastical History, *vol. ii. p.* 270, was plainly a figure of the Pha-
risaical religion, which was only outside shew; and of the rejection and
fall of the Jewish nation.

"† Some cavillers at Christianity," says Gilbert Wakefield, "have made
great objections to this miracle of our Saviour, and have asked, what
right he had to destroy this fig-tree. Now it is sufficient to observe, in
answer to this cavil, that the tree appears to have been barren, and therefore of no *use* to any one; and that it could hardly be private property,
because it grew in the *high road.* (ἐπι της ὁδυ)"—*See his Commentary on
St. Matthew, p.* 296.

‡ See Hammond's works, *vol iii. p.* 168—Annot. on St. Mark.

" *If any man come to me, and hate not his father and mother, and wife and children, and brethren and sisters, yea, and his own life also, he cannot be my disciple.*" *Luke xiv. 26.*

EVERY thing in our religion, has undoubtedly a reference to a future life. It is, therefore, the supreme concern of the pious believer, to please God in all his thoughts and actions. But surely, if we were compelled to interpret literally this sentence, we should see just cause to object to the morality of the Gospel, and its suitableness as well to the government of mankind, as to the exercise of the best affections of our nature. In those words, Jesus then could only be considered as saying, that, if you do not prefer me to those with whom you are bound in the dearest domestic ties; if my doctrines are not able to draw off your attention from the things of this world, and to affix them on those above; you must not hope to be ranked among the number of my disciples*. Perhaps, also, as the

---

* By 'hating,' our Lord does not mean the passion of the mind so called, but an inferior consideration, and regard, such a forsaking of the nearest relations, and such an exposing of life to the rage of persecution, as resembled *the effects* of hatred. All must perceive that this sacrifice of worldly connections, this severe self-denial, and daily danger of death, were peculiar to the times when the rancour of the Jews and Heathens was so hot against the first preachers of the Gospel.—*See Archbishop Newcombe's Observations on our Lord's conduct, p. 44.*

High Priest was a type of our Lord, and as it was considered, according to Philo Judæus*, his duty to put off all natural affection for his father and mother, children and brothers, if it interfered with the service of God, Jesus might have looked to that maxim, when he made the above declaration.

" And the Lord commended the unjust Steward because he had done wisely."—Luke xvi. 8.

It is the characteristic mark of excellence in the parables of our Saviour, to be alike adapted to the comprehension of the ignorant and prejudiced, for whom they were originally designed, and at the same time equally fitted for the instruction of the most learned and judicious. Yet, the friends of religion cannot help observing, that men, of heated imaginations, have been led, by this figurative manner of composition, into the most extravagant expositions, and thereby have furnished irreligious persons with a plausible pretext to object against an unnecessary obscurity in

* Προσκεκληρωμενος Θεω, και της ιερας ταξεως γεγονως ταξιαρχος, οφειλει παντων αλλοτριουσθαι των εν γενεσει, μη γονεων, μη τεκνων, μη αδελφων ευνοιας ολως επιλωμενος, ως η παρελθειν η υπερθεσθαι τι των οσιων. *See his Treatise de Monarch. Lib.* ii. *p.* 230.

some discourses of our Saviour, which they eagerly insinuate to be inconsistent with his wisdom and goodness. The above parable is one therefore which profane cavillers have never failed to select, as it is remarkable for the extreme difficulty of its solution, and sus-
ceptible of the most perverse and dangerous mis-
construction.

To offer a suitable explanation of it then, will be an
attempt perfectly according with the professed object
of this essay. In the first place, we must point out
to the attention of our readers, that Jesus, aware of the
improper inferences that might be drawn from this parable, without an immediate explication of it, did not
suffer the multitude to depart, as he did upon some
other similar occasions, but directly shewed to them
the uses and reflexions which were to be gathered from
the story; and the true moral and design of the parable
in the master's commending the criminal scheme of
his servant, is to prove to us, how the conduct of wicked,
as well as of good men, may supply us with the most
important instruction; for the failings and imperfections of the one, call on us as much for our avoid-
ance, as we are bound to imitate what is praise-worthy
in the other. To imagine that the unjust steward
is held up to us as a pattern for imitation, in any

other sense, would be subjecting this parable to the
charge of countenancing the practice of fraud and injustice in the most extensive degree. Properly speaking, however, the approbation of his Lord did not
extend to the action or to the actor, but was solely confined to the ingenuity of his device; for it is worthy of
remembrance, that he still gives him the title of *the
unjust steward.* As the steward then provided houses
where he might be received upon his dismissal, by secretly making considerable abatements of the debts
which his master's tenants owed for their possessions;
so ought we, as our Lord most forcibly inculcates, to
imitate his provident care for his future interest, by
exerting ourselves with the same vigilance and solicitude, to obtain an everlasting habitation in Heaven,
which can only be done, by the employment of our
riches to such honourable purposes, as may be conducive to future and eternal happiness.

---

*" Jesus saith unto her, Woman, what have I to do with
thee, mine hour is not yet come."—John ii. 4.*

THIS answer is particularized by some, as inconsistent with that affectionate and dutiful respect, which

divines affirm, was uniformly shewn by Jesus towards his parents. But it must proceed from a very ignorant interpretation of the word Woman, to infer that our Lord, by the use of it to his mother, was deficient in filial respect and submission. For though that appellation now carries an aspect of coarseness and vulgarity, yet, in ancient times, it was applied to females the most illustrious in rank and descent, as may be proved in an hundred instances from the Greek writers*. There is something, therefore, more plausible in the way which many apologize for Jesus calling his mother, Woman, when they say, that he thus addressed her, in order that she might remember certain passages which must impress her with sentiments of the highest reverence towards him, on account of his miraculous birth: yet those who offer this explanation, do surely forget that our Saviour used the same expression in recommending his mother on

---

* The classical reader will remember, that Antenor addresses Helen by the appellation of γυαι; and that in Xenophon's Cyropæd. *(Lib. v. p.* 317, Edit. Hutch.) a Persian chief, when trying to console a captive of the highest rank, under her unfortunate circumstances, says, Θαρσει, ὦ γυναι,—take courage, woman. In like manner, as Wetslein observes, Dion. Cass. in Hist. Rom. *p.* 351, makes the Emperor Augustus say to Cleopatra, Θαρσει, ὦ γυναι, και Θυμον ἐχε ἀγαθον,—take courage, woman, and have a good heart.—In imitation of the Greeks, Horace calls Livia, Mulier,—*Carm.* iii. *p.* 14, 15.

the cross, with the utmost filial tenderness, to the care of his favourite disciple, "*Woman, behold thy son.*"

"*And he that was dead came forth, bound hand and foot with grave-cloths, and his face was bound about with a napkin. Jesus saith unto them, loose him, and let him go.*" John xi. 44.

AMID the many strokes which have been aimed against the invincible shield of Christianity, we are not surprised that those who have attempted to bring the historical part of it into discredit, should put this insulting question upon the resurrection of Lazarus: How could a man come out of his grave, who was bound hand and foot? That accurate and intelligent traveller, Maundrell*, will, perhaps assist us, in a great measure, to illustrate this very important question. From him we learn, that the Jews did not, in general, make use of coffins in burying their dead, but placed the bodies in niches, cut into the sides of caves or rooms, hewn out of rocks. We are not, therefore, to understand St. John as saying, that Lazarus

* See Description of the Sepulchre of the Kings, in his Journey from Aleppo, &c. p. 76, 77.

walked out of the sepulchre, but that, extended on his back in a niche, he raised himself in a sitting posture, and then putting his legs over the edge of his niche or cell, slid down, and stood upright on the floor. Now it is very clear, that this might be easily effected, notwithstanding his arms were pinioned, as it were, to his body, and his legs fastened together with the shroud and rollers*. The order, therefore, which Jesus gave, for him to be unbound, very naturally followed the performance of this stupendous miracle†.

———

" *And when he had thus said, he breathed on them, and saith unto them, Receive ye the Holy Ghost.*"—*John xx.* 22.

THESE words at the first glance have perplexed some, into whose minds the awful truths of the Gospel have deeply sunk. Our Lord, it is well known, al-

* In consequence of the difficulty of supposing that the body of Lazarus was so involved, that he could not readily come forth from the tomb, some commentators have imagined it to be more probable, that the body was only slightly wrapped in a large linen cloth, tied at the hands and feet. —*See Ellsley's Annotations on the Four Gospels, Vol. ii. p.* 474.

† The Evangelist, observes Lightfoot, seems so particular in mentioning the grave cloths wherewith Lazarus was bound hand and foot, as also the napkin that had covered his face, on purpose to hint to us *a second miracle in this great miracle.*—*Vol. ii. p.* 583.

ways speaks of the Holy Ghost as not being to come till he should have risen from the dead, and be exalted to the right hand of the Father. Yet, some days before that great event had taken place, he says to his disciples, " *Receive ye the Holy Ghost.*" This apparent difficulty may be thus reconciled. It is very evident, in the first place, that Christ was to bestow the gift of the Holy Ghost upon his disciples, not in the character of a prophet, but as the eternal Sovereign of the Church. The reason, therefore, of his saying, in the present tense, " Receive ye the Holy Ghost," must be taken in the prophetic style, as a thing they should soon receive, as certainly as he breathed upon them[*], In the same manner as he says,—" This is my body, which is broken for you—This is the New Testament in my blood, which is shed for you—Now is the Son of man glorified."

[*] Confirming, says Bishop Pearce, by this outward act, (his breathing on them,) the promise which he had made that they should receive it; as they soon afterwards did. *See Acts, chap. ii. v. 2, 3.—John, chap. vii. v.* 39.—This does not mean the actual imparting of the Holy Ghost, but a solemn promise confirmed by breathing on them, expressive of a sacred spirit or breath, το πνευμα, to fit them for the reception at a proper time.—*Ellsley's Annotations on the Four Gospels, vol. ii.* p. 535, 536.

WE have now briefly touched upon those injunctions and actions of our Lord, to which such, whose hearts and minds are under the influence of prepossession and prejudice against the Scriptures, and such, whose religious doubts may be said to proceed from want of information, have equally raised objections. The true christian, however, will not look upon the New Testament with less reverence, because he cannot understand all its contents; he knows that his life is a life of faith as well as of practice: to believe only, then, that which is inducible to his reason, he is aware is not truth, but mere philosophy: he, therefore, deems it as foolish, as it is presumptuous, to disbelieve what he cannot account for*; being perfectly satisfied, that what materially concerns him to know, is so obvious and express, that it can be equally understood by the lowest as by the highest capacities; namely, that by the intervention of Jesus Christ, he and all mankind will obtain eternal happiness, if they love and obey him.

---

* It is indeed a capital error, in the study of Holy Scripture, not to take the revealed word to be the rule of our implicit belief. And to those who will not give their assent to any doctrines but what they can perfectly comprehend, we may say with the same propriety as St. Austin did to the Manichæans, *Aperte discite non vos credere Christi evangelio, nam qui in evangelio quod vultis creditis, vobis potius quam evangelio creditis.—Contra Faust. Lib. xvii. cap. 3.*

ESSAY III.

ON THE DIFFICULTY OF A MEMBER OF PARLIAMENT BELONGING TO NO PARTY.

FEW questions, perhaps, have been more agitated by
the higher classes of politicians, than the possibility of
a Member of Parliament maintaining so complete a
state of independence, as to support or oppose no measure, but from principles the most impartial and con-
scientious : but, though this be one of those questions which can never be finally set at rest, until one
uniform opinion shall prevail, respecting the nature
and spirit of our constitution (the best, with all its defects, that was ever formed by human wisdom); yet,
it may not be uninteresting to enquire, what good
consequences are likely to result from a representative
of the people in parliament standing aloof from all
political connexions.

We must, however, presuppose, in the first place,
that the member who chalks out for himself this rare
line of conduct, and invariably pursues it, is gifted

with those intellectual qualities, which at once inspire confidence, and command admiration; or else his influence can be but little felt, in the hoarse din of factions, however deservedly his private virtues may be the theme of general panegyric. To be irresistibly impelled, by a love of justice and a regard for worth, into a contest against those, with whom we have lived in habits of intimacy and friendship, may be regarded perhaps, as one of the greatest efforts of patriotism. Such generous devotion to the public service, is, indeed, so seldom witnessed, that, when an orator seizes every opportunity to proclaim his resolution of upholding the liberties of the people, and of acquiescing in no measure, directly or indirectly, but such as is essentially connected with the well-being of the state, much less to enter, from party principles, into a systematic opposition to the measures of government,—we are apt to hear those protestations with a sneer of derision, and to suspect, that he has no other aim in promulging them, than the selfish, but very natural one, of obtaining a place and emolument.

He must give, then, proofs the most undeniable, that he is sincere and steadfast in his great undertaking, before we can be persuaded, that no motive, but a firm conviction of the moral benefit and commendable example he shall impart to others, could have pricked him on to stand forth as a candidate for the illustrious title of a real patriot ; and, even when we are thoroughly satisfied, that he will not betray the hopes reposed in him, what dangers has he to encounter, what passions to subdue, what intrigues to baffle, what temptations to withstand, what factions to crush, and what scurrility, private as well as public, to endure, in his political capacity, before the extent of his herculean toil can be properly appreciated, and his reputation be commensurate to it ! No wonder, then, that men possessing birth, fortune, talents of various kinds, and the most spirited dispositions, should yet prefer the shackles of party, to such a perilous and discouraging post of duty, as that unquestionably is, of equally opposing the court and the people, whenever the views of either are marked by injustice. The difficulties of sustaining the character of a true patriot for any continuance of time, being of such a complexion as to be considered almost unsurmountable*, let us proceed to form some estimate of the ge-

* Some desponding spirits are inclined to think, that we have entered into a sort of confederacy against all public virtue, and that in this age, it is as rare to meet with a real patriot, as it was formerly to meet with a poet in Plato's commonwealth. There are doubtless too many who assume the external appearance of the patriot, without having any of

neral good likely to be communicated, from a man pursuing a line of conduct so worthy of the most lasting veneration and gratitude.

If we could concur in opinion with those, whose indiscriminate zeal for a reform in parliament has led them to go the unwarrantable length of asserting, that the House of Commons is almost composed of placemen, pensioners, and purchasers of boroughs, it must be obvious, that a single voice, however eloquent and independent, could not possess the smallest weight in an assembly filled with persons of such a servile character: but the fact, fortunately for us, is far from being so. There are many, doubtless, in the House of Commons, who suffer their interests to lead them from their duty; yet it is equally indisputable, that no act of public rapacity, despotism, or infringement upon the constitution, can be committed, but some will be found in that assembly*, to avow their indignation, and call aloud for vengeance.

its constituent qualities. But the names of *Whitbread, Romilly, and Wilberforce,* awaken recollections highly favorable to the belief, that there are men still to be found who entertain an invincible and instinctive hatred of oppression, and an unshaken love of liberty both civil and religious.

* "Like Noah's ark," says an old writer, "clean and unclean animals enter into the House of Commons."

When a member of parliament has succeeded in acquiring for himself the rare fame of forming the most impartial judgment concerning the real character and tendency of public measures, and, consequently, of disdaining to be enlisted under the banners of any faction, occasions may arise, where such integrity and public spiritedness will produce effects the most import-ant to the national peace, prosperity, and happiness: for though it may not be safe to lay it down as a position, without much reserve and limitation, that an assembly like that of the House of Commons, is often governed by the impulse of one mind, unless the possessor of it has, at the same time, the office of prime minister, yet the memorable decision passed upon the slave trade, clearly demonstrates to us, that one who was never called upon to dispense the favours of the crown, was yet able, from the firmly-established opinion, that, in his long public career, he did every thing according to principle, and nothing according to party, to stop the progress of corruption in its worst of forms, and to retrieve the character of the nation, by exalting the hitherto persecuted and enslaved Africans, into the scale of free and rational beings*.

* In offering these sentiments, I would not wish to be thought blind to the good intentions of *some ministers,* or less ready than others, to

In another point of view, the character of the member of parliament, who equally enjoys the respect of the government and the confidence of the public, may be contemplated, as operating upon the spirit of the latter, and giving it a right direction, where otherwise it would have slept, or been crushed. When a king wishes to enlarge the prerogative, or a minister covets a power which the constitution denies him, the good effects of that happy confidence will be more extensive, than it may be, perhaps, at first conceived. Should the House of Commons defeat the great purposes of its representation, by manifesting no other virtue than pliability, no other policy than self-interest, the true patriot will never sit down satisfied, until he has succeeded in unfolding to the public eye all those secret ministerial springs, whereby so many free agents are converted into mere machines, or into mutes, whose sole and degrading office it is, to stand

render justice to their respective merits. Such indeed is the *delicate situation* of *all ministers*, that every candid mind is disposed to put the most favourable construction upon acts, which otherwise might often seem to demand the severest reprehension. A great poet has thus finely characterized their peculiar situation :—

> Our ministers like gladiators live;
> 'Tis half their business, blows to ward or give :
> The good their virtue would effect, or sense,
> Dies between exigence and self defence.

53

like a drove of oxen, to be counted on a division*.
But to undo link by link, and open spring by spring,
is an operation of such nice and delicate nature, as can
only be completely executed by the hand of the master workman. That being accomplished, the people
are prepared to enforce by practice, the principles
which have been so strongly impressed on their
minds. They are awakened to a strict attention to the
conduct of their representatives; and all the substantial checks which they can employ, are put in use, to
bring back the constitution to its true principles; nor
do they ever cease persevering, when thus their spirit
and intelligence are called forth, until they have perfectly attained their ends. By such means, a whole
nation has been, and may be again, moved and animated by one individual. Thus, has the column of
public freedom been made to stand upon a firmer basis,

* It is a remark too common to be untrue, that the instances *there*,
are very frequent of persons having a "*political palsy*" *in the head*,
nodding and assenting to all. It would be an invidious task to enquire
into the causes of *this complaint.* It is sufficient for our humiliation
that we feel the effects. They would however do well to remember, that
this sort of obsequious dulness may be highly prudent in a state where
it is dangerous to be honest, and only profitable to be vicious; but in a
government like ours, distinguished above all others for its freedom and
greatness, it may produce, in the end, consequences highly injurious to
its *liberty, prosperity, and happiness.*

E

when its superstructure was, perhaps, on the point of being diminished.

The man, who so essentially contributes to promote the happiness, and to secure the liberties of his fellow citizens, without having the wish or hope to obtain the seals of office, will not, however, be so intoxicated with the general applause and admiration which, under such circumstances, must accompany his footsteps, as to sacrifice that high respect and gratitude he has gained in the breasts of sober and reflecting minds, to the vain and precarious favour of the multitude; but, on the contrary, will still remain inspired, as he was before, with the same real love of true glory, and with the same real dislike of popular fame. " *Est enim gloria, solida quædam res expressa non adumbrata; ea est consentiens laus bonorum, incorrupta vox bene judicantium de excellente virtute. Ea virtuti resonat tanquam imago gloriæ. Quæ quia recte factorum plerumque comes est, non est bonis viris repudianda. Illa autem quæ se ejus imitatricem esse vult, temeraria atque inconsiderata, et plerumque peccatorum vitiorumque laudatrix fama popularis, simulatione honestatis, formam ejus pulchritudinemque corrumpit*.*"

* Cicero Tuscul. Quæst. Lib. iii.

ESSAY IV.

ON THE CONDITION AND CHARACTER OF WOMEN IN
DIFFERENT COUNTRIES AND AGES.

IF the enlightened among our sex have rejoiced that
they were born in a period of high civilization, how
much greater cause have those of the other, to congra-
tulate themselves upon the same event; since in polished nations, it is rarely the hard fate of women to
be first adored, and then oppressed. We do not begin by being their slaves, and end in becoming their
tyrants: for when the transient charms of youth
and beauty fade, in the place of our idols, we make
them our companions and friends.

In rude periods of society, woman is treated with the
utmost coolness, indifference, contempt, and tyranny:
the savage regards her only as a being of inferior species, and, consequently, with him, love is nothing but
a simple instinct of nature, which he disdains, however, to procure by any of those arts which are calculated to win affection and favour. It is the opinion of
the great Bacon, that love is the first of human plea-

sures, and intoxication the second. The justness of this observation is disputed by the Indians of America; according to whose philosophy, intoxication is the greatest of human pleasures. It may be advanced, as another proof of the contempt and servitude in which women are held by savages, that, in their drunken assemblies, females are allowed to be present only for the menial and degrading purpose of supplying the liquor, and taking care of their sovereigns, when their reason is extinguished. Among the American tribes, the condition of women may be compared, indeed, to that of the Helotes among the Spartans, a vanquished race, doomed to pass their whole life in administering to the wants of their conquerors. The rigorous despotism exercised by barbarians over the female sex, will be found to constitute their general character, in almost every quarter of the globe.

If we turn our eyes towards the eastern nations, to Turkey, Persia, Mogul, Japan, and the Empire of China, we shall see women reduced to the same state of slavery. Asia, from time immemorial, may be regarded as a vast and dreary prison, for the reception of female beauty. The cursed spirit of despotism is, indeed, as fatal to love, as to virtue: exposed to all the caprices of a master, ·who looks upon female beauty as subservient to the purposes of animal enjoyment only, the will of the unhappy object of his lust must be his; since resistance in the Harem would be fatal, and flight from it impossible.

Plutarch, in speaking of the Persians, has noticed the severe treatment of their wives, in such terms as would justify us in concluding that it equally met with his disapprobation and that of his countrymen; but the domestic institutions of the Greeks inform us, that the notions they entertained of the female character, were scarcely more just and liberal than those of the people whom the philosopher of Cheronœa styles barbarians. The Greek, like the Persian women, were excluded from society, and shut up in sequestered apartments, and when they left them to go abroad, an indulgence but rarely granted, their faces were covered by veils; while, upon no occasion whatsoever, were they permitted to appear at public entertainments. The wives who had been prolific, experienced, perhaps, a greater portion of liberty than that which fell to the share of the new-married woman, and the virgin; yet still they had just reason to complain of the bolts and bars placed in their chambers by the jealousy or tyranny of their lords*. The possibility, however, of escaping from the hands of. their oppressors, was presented to them by a divorce; but that could not be effected without the consent of both parties. In this manner the wife of Pericles gained her freedom†.

There was a wide contrast, in the condition of the Athenian, and their neighbours the Lacedæmonian, women. The laws of Lycurgus did not establish such a cruel distinction between the sexes, as existed in those of Solon; for they authorized women to quit that privacy which Pericles‡ deemed so essential to the preservation of their character, and to frequent solemn festivals and sacrifices. In their fashions too we may espy the same difference, as in their manners. The Lacedæmonian virgins went abroad with their faces uncovered, while the married women invariably appeared

* —————————— Ταις γυναικωνιτισιν
Σφραγιδας ιπιβαλλωσιν ηδη, και μοχλως
Τηρωντας ημας και προσιλι Μολοτικως
Τριφωσι, μορμολυκεια τοις μοιχοις, κυνας.

See Aristophanis Comæd.—Thesmophor, ver. 414—417.

† See Plutarch in Vita Periclis.

‡ See his Speech in Thucydides, Lib. ii.

with their veils. This custom was defended on the very natural and justifiable principle, of the former wishing to get husbands, and of the latter to keep those which they already possessed. But many will be inclined to think, that their practice of dancing naked, at those entertainments, before a concourse of male spectators, was well suited to encourage a general state of promiscuous intercourse between the sexes. It does, however, appear, that while the Spartans continued to pay that profound veneration to the statutes of their celebrated lawgiver, as to fulfil them without hesitation or reserve, adultery was a crime so rare among them, that no punishment was assigned for it[*]: but when the stern virtues of their ancestors were no longer inscribed upon their minds, the licentiousness of the women arose to such an extravagant pitch, that they

---

[*] In Plutarch, the judge and panegyrist of so many illustrious men, we read that Geradas, a primitive Spartan, being asked by a stranger what punishment their law had for an adulterer? replied, that it would be just as possible to find one in Sparta, as it would be to meet with a bull, whose neck should be so long as to reach over the mountain Taygetas, and drink of the river Eurotas, that lay on the other side.—*See Vita Lycurg.* From this speech, we are not, then, of course, to suppose the invitations which the Spartans were accustomed to give to handsome men, to share the favour of their wives, from the patriotic principle of supplying the state with a robust progeny, are to be ranked under the name of adultery.

were even stigmatized by writers with the epithet ἀνδρομανεῖς*.

In surveying the condition of women in the states of Greece, especially in Athens, our attention cannot fail to be arrested by the pomp and splendour assumed by the courtezans, and the honours to which they openly aspired, and which they received; while the married females, as we have already shewn, were subjected to the most mortifying inferiority, and esteemed only worthy to perform the meanest functions of domestic œconomy. Various causes have been suggested to account for that curious and important fact; but the following perhaps will be admitted by the philosopher as the most satisfactory and conclusive.

It is well known, that in many of the Greek colonies of Asia, temples were erected to Venus, in which voluptuousness and superstition equally concurred, not only to protect harlots, but even to raise them to the rank of priestesses of that meritricious divinity. In Grecian story, the people of Corinth were noted even to a proverb, for indulging their sensual passions without reserve; and that city was the first which in-

---

* This term, which may be interpreted, running mad after men, strongly paints the unbounded lasciviousness of the Spartan women. It was given them by Euripides, and is cited by Plutarch in Vita Numæ.

troduced a colony of those aspiring females from the East. We are told by an historian*, whose authority is deservedly of great weight, that Corinth could number at one time a thousand females, who prostituted their charms for hire+ in the temple of the goddess of beauty. Upon the efficacy of their prayers to Venus, these strumpets seem to place the firmest reliance; for they had recourse to them in every situation of difficulty and danger. Miltiades and Themistocles were even supposed to have become the saviours of Greece, because these votaries of lust‡ had invoked their tutelary deity for the success of their armies.

---

* See Strabo, Lib. viii. p. 581.

+ Οὐ παντος ἀνδρος ἰς Κορινθον ἰσθ'ὁ πλως,—This proverb, so common in Greece, which Horace has thus translated, " Non cuivis hominum contingit adire Corinthum," is generally supposed to have taken its rise from some of these harlots admitting none to their embraces, but those who could afford to pay the most exorbitant price. It is recorded that Demosthenes visited Corinth for the express purpose of passing a night with the famous strumpet Laïs : but the enormous tax which she exacted for that pleasure, ten thousand drachmas, in our money about three hundred pounds, produced this exclamation from the mouth of the orator, ὀκ, ἐταιμαι μυριων δραχμων μεταμελειαν. See Aulus Gellius, Noctes Atticæ, Lib. I. cap. viii.

‡ The magistrates of that republic even ordered their portraits to be painted at the public expence, in gratitude for their powerful intercessions.—See Athenæi Deipnosophist. Lib xiii.

This class of women were even associated to religion, by the arts. The famous Phryné, who had amassed such a treasure by the free use of her captivating person, as to have proposed taking upon herself the whole expence of re-building* the walls of Thebes, which had been demolished by Alexander, served as a model to the great masters of sculpture and painting, Praxiteles and Apelles, for their most unrivalled productions. Her exquisite beauty is said to have inspired the former with the idea of his Cnidian Venus, so rapturously extolled by Lucian+, and for the possession of which, Nicomedes, king of Bithynia, in vain offered to discharge the immense debts of that republic‡: and the celebrated picture of Venus Anadyomene, which adorned the temple of Æsculapius, in the island

* Provided, however, that the following unparalleled inscription was placed on them :—*Alexander diruit, sed meretrix Phryné refecit;* but it was refused.—*See Pliny, Lib. xxxiv. cap.* 8.—*Lib. xxxvii. cap.* 5.

+ See Lucian, in the Ερωτης. The illusion of the Greeks was so great with this celebrated production, says that writer, that they fancied the marble moved, that it seemed to speak, and they ended by applying their lips to those of the Goddess.—*See likewise the Anthologia, cap. xi. xii. xiii.* upon this subject.

‡ See Pausanias, Lib. i. cap. 40.—Lib. viii. cap. 9. and Pliny, lib. vii. cap. 34.

of Cos*, was undertaken by the latter, from having seen Phryné on the sea-shore, with no other covering than her long and floating tresses. The greater part of the courtezans were likewise musicians; and in an art so much admired in Greece†, and so well adapted to inflame and nourish every voluptuous passion, and consequently, so deeply connected with their own interests and fame, we can readily believe their skill to have been prodigious.

It is also known, how grateful the sight of beauty

---

* The supposed place where Apelles was born : but Augustus afterwards obtained this incomparable painting, and remitted to the inhabitants as an equivalent for it, the sum of three hundred talents, upon the tribute which they owed to his exchequer.—" Φασι δι τοις Κωοις αντι της γραφης ικατον ταλαντων αφισιν γινεσθαι τα προσταχθεντος φορα."—*See Strabo, lib. xiv.*—Athenæus asserts, that both those famous productions, the picture as well as the statue, were copied after the courtezan Phryné. The celebrated statue of the Venus de Medicis is likewise supposed by many connoisseurs, to be only a copy of the Venus of Cnidus.

† The use of the flute formed part of the education of the young Athenians, previous to the Peloponnesian war ; but conceiving that that instrument marred their beauty, (a circumstance to which they were uncommonly attentive,) by communicating a disagreeable protuberance to their lips and cheeks, it was condemned and abandoned by the general consent of the nation. Omnium tum Atheniensium consensu disciplina tibiis canendi desita est.—*Vide Aulus Gellius, Lib. xv. cap.* 17.—From similar motives, perhaps, Plato banished the Bœotian flute from his republic, and preferred the lyre or cithern for schools of music.

was to the Greeks, and how often they were the dupes and instruments of it in their military and civil transactions. Enthusiastic in all their feelings, the ardent souls and inflammable imaginations of this people adored beauty in the temples, admired it in master-pieces of the arts*, contemplated it in the games and exercises, and gave prizes to it in the public festivals: but the restraint and seclusion in which the married women, especially among the Athenians, were kept, and the incessant toil and drudgery to which they were exposed, extinguished in them all solicitude to set off whatever natural beauty they possessed to the greatest advantage. That homage, therefore, which they ought, and would have received, if they had not been excluded by the law from cultivating a refinement of taste and manners, by mixing in society†, was necessarily engrossed by the courtezans, who, fettered by no occupations of that kind, were left at full leisure to study every captivating variety of dress, and to heighten the effect of their personal charms by a display of

* See Wincklemann Histoire de l' Art. chez les Anciens.—*Tom. II. Liv. iv. cap. 2.*

† Except for the purpose of attending a procession or a funeral, (*see Lysiæ Orationes, pro cæde Erastothenis Defensio, p. 3.*) they were scarcely ever permitted to appear abroad, as we have before observed.

all those accomplishments, which can engage and delight. The courtezans of Athens lived in a public manner; and to their entertainments, orators, philosophers and poets, and all who were eminent in any department of art or science, constantly repaired, for the sake of those qualities, that were so attractive. Thus they imparted to the men of letters, an elegance of manners, a playfulness of wit, and turn of pleasantry delicately ironical; while they, in return, by occasionally frequenting their schools, gained from them an elevation and enlargement of mind, which rendered their conversation brilliant in the highest degree.

Among this meretricious class, there was one who acquired such an ascendency over superior minds, as even to become the object of public consideration. The name of the celebrated Aspasia, the mistress of Pericles, will here, doubtless, present itself to the recollection of the classical reader. She is said to have been born at Miletus, the chief town of Ionia; and such was the combination of extraordinary endowments found in her, that the historians who have recorded her praises seem to be undetermined whether she most excelled in her person or in her mind. The grave and enlightened Socrates was mute and attentive when she spoke; and Pericles placed such confidence in her judgment, as to consult her on all state matters of great moment. Plato, whose character for sagacity and political knowledge was equalled by few, and surpassed by none, of his contemporaries, hesitates not to pay her the remarkable compliment of saying, that her instructions contributed powerfully to form the greatest and most eloquent orators of her age*; while Plutarch+, although inclined to consider her as the author of the Peloponnesian war, and to stigmatize her licentiousness with a manly indignation, relates, as an indisputable proof of her deep skill in the science of politics, that one Lysicles, by attaching himself to her society, after the death of Pericles, arose from the meanest origin and education to the first employment in the republic. So various and splendid, indeed, were her attainments, that they seem to have communicated a degree of glory to her profligate profession: yet, we cannot help thinking, there is too much exaggeration in the remark, that her example and instruction rendered Athens the school of vice and pleasure, when it is stated, at the same time,

* See Harpocration voce Aspasia.—Plato in Menexeno.

+ See Vita Periclis.

to have been the custom for husbands to bring their wives to her house, to be instructed by her discourses; although they were perfectly aware, it was not less a seminary for prostitution than for oratory*. They, therefore, who could treat their wives with such unprecedented indelicacy and disrespect, must surely be considered, by all impartial judges, to complain with a very ill grace of the dissoluteness of Aspasia and her companions.

These reasons will serve to account for the homage which courtezans so often received in Greece. Without them, we should indeed but darkly comprehend why they became the objects of such excessive admiration to orators, philosophers, poets, painters, and statuaries; why Phryné had a statue of gold at Delphi, placed between the statues of two kings; and why some of them, after their death, should be honoured with splendid monuments. The traveller, in his ap-

---

* Upon this circumstance, which is so singular, that we safely pronounce it to be without a parallel in the history of any other people of antiquity, Plutarch expresses himself in the clearest terms:—" Τας γυναικας ἀκροασομενας ὁι συνηθεις ἠγον ιις αὐτην, και περ ὑ κοσμιυ προιξυ(αι ἐργασιας, ὑδι σεμνης ἀλλα παιδισκας ἑταιρυσας τρεφυσαν."—See *Vita Periclis*. The latter part of this assertion is confirmed by Athenæus:—Και Ασπασια δι ἡ Σωκρατικη ἐνεπορευΐο πληθη καλων γυναικων και ἐπληθυνεν αὐτο των ταυτης ἑταιριδων ἡ Ἑλλας."—*Lib. xiii.* p. 570.

proach to Athens, says an eminent Greek writer, Dicæarchus*, beholds afar off, a musoleum on the side of the road, which attracts his attention: he conceives it to be the tomb of Miltiades, or of Pericles, or of some other illustrious character who has served his country: he at length draws near to it, and finds it to be, a courtezan of Athens, who is interred with such pomp; and, in a letter to Alexander, Theopompus, speaking of this same mausoleum, emphatically observes, " This distinguished mark of public respect, a courtezan has received; while of all those who perished in Asia, fighting for the general safety of Greece, there is not one whose ashes have received, or even been thought worthy to receive, a similar honour.†" Such was the senseless extravagance, inconsistency, degeneracy, and ingratitude of the Athenians. But these traits were perfectly accordant with the character of a people who could banish Themistocles, starve Aristides, poison Socrates‡, prefer

* This enlightened and impartial Greek was the disciple of Aristotle, and wrote some years after the death of Alexander.

† Apud Athenæum.

‡ Well might Valerius Maximus exclaim on contemplating the monstrous injustice of this state to its benefactors,—Felices Athænas, quæ post

the licentious buffoonery of Aristophanes, to the sublime and pathetic compositions of Sophocles, and Euripides*; reverence the sanctity of marriage, and yet suffer themselves to be governed by Aspasia, and her school of harlots†.

illorum exilium. invenire aliquem aut virum bonum aut amantem sui civem potuerunt.—Lib. v. cap. 3.

* It is a matter of just surprise, that the Athenians had not possessed a more correct taste, when we consider that they were so exceedingly fond of dramatic entertainments, as to have several trajedies performed at one sitting: although Aristotle's supposition (in his Poetics) of a hundred trajedies being performed in concurrence, must pass for an *exuberantia orationis*, to use the expression of a learned critic.

† From Miss Lucy Aikin's *Epistles on the character and condition of Women in various ages and countries*, which we think no one can peruse without receiving a strong impression of the lofty genius and delicate taste of the writer, the following beautiful passage in her rapid view of the state of Athens, may here be quoted with the utmost propriety:—

> Graced by the sword, the chisel, and the pen,
> Athens! illustrious seat of far-famed men,
> Receive my homage! Hark! what shouts arise
> As Phryné gilds the pomp of sacrifice!
> To Beauty's queen the graceful dance they twine,
> Trill the warm hymn, and dress the flowery shrine ;
> Priestess of love she fills the eager gaze,
> And fires and shares the worship that she pays.
> Haste, sculptor, haste! that form, that heavenly face,
> Catch ere they fade, and fix the mortal grace.
> Phryné in gold shall deck the sacred fane,
> And Pallas' virgin image frown in vain.
> Rise, bright Aspasia too ! thy tainted name
> Sails down secure through infamy to fame ;

Statesman

The condition of the Roman was unquestionably not so grievous as that of the Grecian women : the former were not excluded, like the latter, from all social intercourse ; nor could they complain of their behaviour being so attentively watched, or so severely scrutinized. Yet among the primitive Romans, the matrimonial contract was most unequal on the side of the woman, and can only be regarded in the degrading light of the conjunction of a master with a slave*. For the stern spirt of the laws, gave *them* the right of life and death over their helpless partners ; and in the cases of adultery or intoxication†, the husband, on

> Statesmen and bards and heroes bend the knee,
> Nor blushes Socrates to learn of thee.
> Thy wives, proud Athens! fetter'd and debas'd,
> Listlessly duteous, negatively chaste,
> O vapid summary of a slavish lot !
> They sew, and spin, they die, and are forgot.
> Cease, headlong muse ! resign the dang'rous theme,
> Perish the glory that defies esteem !
> Inspire thy trump at Virtue's call alone,
> And blush to blazon whom she scorns to own.
>
> *See Epistle* iii. *v.* 82—105.

* See Aulus Gellius, Lib. x. Cap. xxiii.

† The same fatal penalty might be inflicted if she even tasted wine without his knowledge. Non licebat vinum fœminis Romanis bibere : invenimus inter exempla Egnatii Mezennii uxorem quod vinum bibisset a dolio interfectam furte enim cædis a Romulo absolutum—*See Pliny, Lib. xiv. Cap. xiv.* Their notion was, that the use of wine provoked amorous passions.

consulting with his friends, might, if he pleased, carry the sentence into execution. Of the coldness and insensibility of the Romans towards their wives, or at least the grossness of their love, a remarkable proof may be cited in the following declaration, which Metellus Numidius made to the Roman people, that, if kind nature had enabled us to do without a wife, we should be delivered from a very troublesome companion: but, since she had so ordered it, that we could neither live with our wives happily enough, nor without them by any means, we must look to matrimony rather for our lasting security, than for a transient gratification*.

Yet still, however, instances can be adduced to shew, that the Romans, in the period under review, treated their wives with some degree of esteem and confidence. Ignorant of arts and pleasures, war and labour were then the chief amusements of a Roman; but after his dangers and toils, he disdained not to partake with his wife in all the cares of domestic life†;

* See Aulus Gellius, Lib. i. cap. vi.

† See the Fourteenth Satire of Juvenal, v. 166—171, for a short, but lively picture, of the simplicity and domestic happiness of the ancient Romans.

and next in estimation to the glory of being honoured by the state for his valour, were the praises it drew from her lips. Nothing, indeed, seems to have been omitted that could inspire the women with a love of virtue and modesty, or dispose them to copy the grave and austere manners of their husbands. A perpetual tutelage, the censure of magistrates, the domestic tri-bunals, the laws to prevent their luxury, by the re-gulation of marriage portions, the sumptuary laws for their ornaments, the temples erected to chastity, the temples to the goddess who presided over the peace of marriages and the appeasement of husbands*, and the honourable decrees for the services which women rendered to the state; all these circumstances evince the deep interest which the Romans manifested in their wives, and in the preservation of their morals.

The Roman women did not exhibit that ferocious courage upon which Plutarch has passed such high en-comiums, in recording the acts of certain Grecian fe-males. Their first virtue was chastity, and their point

* It is justly observed by Gibbon, in his Decline and Fall of the Roman Empire, *vol.* *viii.* *octavo edit. p.* 63, that the epithet of *viriplaca* too clearly indicates on which side submission and repentance were always to be expected.

of honour decency. It is well known, that Cato, the censor, expelled a senator for having kissed his wife in the presence of his daughter. To these austere manners, the Roman women united an unbounded love for their country, which appeared on many striking occasions. Upon the death of Brutus, they clad themselves in deep mourning; and had *they* not supplicated, Rome itself would have been sacrificed to the stern vengeance of Coriolanus. The senate testified their gratitude by a public decree, which assigned to them the exclusive merit of saving their country. In the time of Brennus, their patriotism was also conspicuous, in giving all their gold for the ransom of the city; and after the fatal battle of Cannæ, when Rome had no other treasures left but the virtues of her citizens, they again cónsecrated their most precious ornaments to the service of the state*.

Such examples of public virtue, on the part of the Roman women, doubtless contributed to raise them in the estimation of their husbands: but these facts are

---

* An action which appeared so praise-worthy in the eyes of their countrymen, that from thenceforth it was permitted, by a law, to pronounce funeral orations in honour of women, which, till that time, were peculiar to men.

not sufficient to justify the hasty conclusions of some writers, that the marriage contract among the Romans must be considered in the light of an union of affec-tion as well as of interest between equals, and that, therefore, all the blessings and comforts of domestic love were enjoyed by both parties. In support of this conclusion, we are not ignorant, that they quote the fact of no Roman exercising his privilege of divorce* for the long space of five hundred and twenty years†; and that Spurius Carvilius Ruga, the first person who availed himself of that right, incurred the hatred of his countrymen. But when it is recollected, that the law gave the husband a title to treat his wife with cru-elty and tyranny, and, that upon this account, she carefully avoided affording him any subject for com-plaint, because she was entirely in his power, we are not, surely, to interpret his forbearing to dissolve the union, into a proof of his passionate fondness, or un-feigned respect for her. We, likewise, presume to

---

* Plutarch tells us, that Romulus allowed a husband to divorce his wife, if she had committed adultery, prepared poison, or procured false keys.

† According to Dionysius Halicarnassensis, Lib. ii. p. 93, and Valerius Maximus, Lib. ii. Cap. i.; and five hundred and twenty-three, according to Aulus Gellius, Lib. iv. Cap. iii.

think, that five centuries did not elapse without producing one intance of divorce among the Romans; for it does appear, that the idea of divorce was not altogether unknown even in the time of Coriolanus, as may be inferred from his advice to his wife, when he went into banishment, to marry a man more fortunate than himself: and with respect to the disgrace into which Carvilius fell with the people, for dismissing his wife, we are not to place their disapprobation to the injustice of that act, but to his having divorced her on account of barrenness, by the desire of the censors, to whose interference they, upon occasions of this kind, always evinced the utmost dread and repugnance*.

The custom, also, of lending a wife to a friend, in order that he might have children by her, at once demonstrates the impurity of manners among the Romans, and the small respect and regard which they entertained for the female sex: and this practice, which appears to have prevailed among the old Romans†, was openly countenanced by the younger Cato.

* Montesquieu has ably examined and elucidated this subject, in his Esprit des Loix, Lib. xvi. Cap. xvi.

† We learn from Plutarch, in his comparison of Numa and Lycurgus,

According to Plutarch, the great orator Hortensius, for the purpose of drawing still closer the ties of friendship and intimacy which already existed between him and Cato, applied, in the first place, to have the use of his daughter Porcia, the wife of Bibulus ; but this proposal not being relished by Cato, on the ground of its being the husband's affair, Hortensius had the modest assurance to ask his friend for his own wife Marcia, who then happened to be in a state of pregnancy : when, so far from expressing the least anger or displeasure at this unparalleled request, Cato turned a willing ear to it, and, by consent of Philippus, the father of Marcia, whose interference, in a legal point of view, was necessary, Hortensius thus obtained possession of her person*.

that the former legislator permitted a Roman husband, after his wife had brought him a sufficient number of children, either to make her over to any person who wished to have a family, or to lend her out for a certain time. This last practice was also common among the Greeks. It is well known that Alcibiades enjoyed the person of Xantippe, by the permission of Socrates, her husband; and, in this instance, no symptoms of her refractory temper are said to have been discovered by the philosopher. The classical reader will also remember, that Plato himself, whose system of ethics is, perhaps, more perfect than that of any other heathen moralist, has yet prescribed a community of wives in his plan of a perfect commonwealth.

* See a full account of this transaction, so offensive to modern feelings and delicacy, in Plutarch, Vita Catonis.

This anecdote, recorded of one of the gravest and most virtuous citizens ever produced by the republic of Rome, may be adduced as an incontestible evidence of the unworthy* treatment to which women, even of the highest rank and character, were exposed; and will warrant the assumption, that although the laws and public institutions affected to respect the sanctity of marriage, and to look upon women as the objects of rational esteem and attachment, yet the Romans are the last people among the nations of antiquity who can, with propriety, be said to exhibit a pleasing spectacle of delicacy and morality, in their conjugal passions and connections.

But, about the end of the commonwealth, a remarkable change took place in the condition, taste, and sentiments of the Roman women. The immense wealth which the conquest of so many opulent nations poured into the capital of the empire, paved the way for the appearance of every species of luxury and vice, among both sexes. Women then began to emerge from their domestic confinement, and to shake off the

* The astonishing fact, mentioned by Livy, Lib. viii. Cap. xviii. of one hundred and ninety noble matrons being convicted of the crime of poisoning their husbands, should teach some writers to be less peremptory in their assertions respecting the matrimonial happiness of the women in the early days of the commonwealth.

weight of the matrimonial yoke. New wants and new passions filled their souls; and the loss of reputation, when subservient to the means of promoting their power, and gratifying their love of distinction, never occasioned a painful emotion, much less marred their general felicity. At the slightest offence, the nuptial knot might be untied by either of the parties. Such, indeed, was the facility of separation, that marriage could only be viewed in the degrading light of a transient connection, formed upon the convenient basis of mutual pleasure and profit. Even those who aspired to be contemplated by the people as models of purity and virtue, hesitated not to indulge themselves in the unlimited freedom of divorce. Marcus Brutus repudiated his wife Claudia, although her fidelity was unquestionable. Cicero acted in the same manner by his wife Terentia, with whom he had lived for thirty years[*]; and we are told, it was afterwards her miserable or happy lot to receive the embraces of three successive husbands; the first of whom was the historian Sallust, who, from that time, is said to have declared

---

[*] In extenuation, however, of this apparently ungenerous treatment, it must be remembered, that she was suspected of having violated the honour of his bed, during his exile in Asia.

himself the implacable enemy of Cicero*. This species of legal prostitution, for well does the nature of
the marriage union of the Romans, at this period,
merit such an appellation, must have prompted Julius
Cæsar to meditate that licentious law, which was to
have granted to him the exclusive liberty of possessing a seraglio of wives+. In short, it might be reasonably supposed, that the Romans of both sexes had
then attained the highest pitch of debauchery, if we
could cease to forget the scenes of unbounded luxury
and lust displayed after the establishment of monarchy.

Under the emperors, the great inequality of ranks,
the outrageous abuse of riches, the ridicule attached to
every law of decency and morality, the ungovernable
fury with which the higher orders of women abandoned themselves alike to their cruel and sensual passions, and the frequent practice of the most unnatural
vices and crimes, could not fail to bring on the matu-

* From what cause we are at a loss to determine; but it is certain
that his veracity as an historian is justly impeached, for omitting several
actions in his relation of Catiline's conspiracy, which reflected the highest
honour upon the first husband of Terentia.

+ Helvius Cinna Trib. pleb, plerisque confessus est habuisse scriptam
paratamque legem, quam Cæsar ferre jussisset, cum ipse abesset, uti
uxores liberores quærendorum causa, quas et quot vellet ducere liberet.—
Suetonius, in Julio, Cap. lii.

rity of depravation. We may conceive at once the perfection of vice to which the women had arrived, even in the time of Augustus, and the secret contempt and disgust with which they had inspired those who participated in their favours, from that remarkable declaration in the speech* which he made to press the Romans to marriage: that the rewards which he had offered to induce them to resign their fondness for a life of celibacy, were of such a magnitude, that thousands would be happy to hazard their lives in the prospect of attaining them; yet for those rewards, when offered as incentives to marriage, none would step forth to receive them. Armed, as Augustus was, with despotic power, yet, after a long struggle, he felt his design of enforcing the bonds of marriage so unpopular, that he was obliged to renounce it as hopeless and impracticable+: so common, indeed, was the infidelity of the wife under him and his successors, that Valerius Maximus, who lived in the reign of Tiberius, assures us, that men were induced to marry from the sole consideration of enriching themselves by the forfeiture of the wife's dower, when she committed

* See his discourse in Dion. Cassius, Lib. lvi.

+ See Suetonius in Augusto, Cap. xxxiv.

adultery*. In his profligate age, we also learn, that a great number of women of condition were not ashamed to present themselves publicly before their Ædiles, in order to be inscribed in the list of courtezans, and to break down, by their own infamy, that barrier which the laws had in vain opposed to their prostitution†: while Seneca declares, that some of the most exalted rank were accustomed to compute their years, not by the number of consuls, but of husbands‡.

From that period, to the accession of Septimus Severus, the utmost lines of vice may be delineated in the conduct of the Roman women : the high and low born were involved in one general course of prostitution§ : every pleasure which did not violate the rules of decency and virtue, was deemed trivial and unmeaning. The Roman ladies then took great pleasure in witnessing the masculine exercises of fencers, and

---

* Valer Maximus, Lib. vi. cap. iii.

† See Tacitus Annalia, Lib. ii. Cap. lxxxv.

‡ Non consulum numero, sed maritorum annos suos computant.— De Beneficiis, Lib. iii. cap. xvi.

§ Iamque eadem summis pariter minimisque libido ;
 Nec melior silicem pedibus quæ conterit atrum
 Quam quæ longorum vehitur cervice Syrorum.
 Juvenal, Sat. vi. v. 348—350.

the fatal combats of gladiators. So enamoured were
they with these bloody sports, and so completely insensible to the delicacy of their sex, and the decorum
of their character, as even to break forth into a rapture
of savage delight*, when the favourite gladiator struck
his antagonist the decisive blow. The rage for spectacles also seized them in the intervals of lust. The
tragic or the comic actor was, in their eyes, an object
worthy of the most passionate attachment: a flute
player swallowed up patrimonies, and gave heirs to
the descendants of the Scipios and Emiliuses; and the
life of a husband was not so estimable as that of a lap-
dog†. Lost to all sense of shame and feeling, the hideous art of procuring abortions was brought to the
summit of perfection‡: and, in the madness of their

---

* —————— ————— Consurgit ad ictus,
*Et quoties victor ferrum jugulo inserit, illa
Delicias ait esse suas*, pectusque jacentis
Virgo *modesta* jubet, converso pollice, rumpi.

Vide Prudentius de Vertalibus.

† Morte viri cupient animam servare catellæ.—*Sat. vi. v.* 653.

‡ Sed jacet aurato vix ulla puerpera lecto
Tantum artes hujus, tantum medicamina possunt,
Quæ steriles facit, atque homines in ventre necandos,
Conducit,————

Sat. vi. v. 593—596.

lewd and capricious passions, the slaves of high-born females were transformed into those monsters of Asia, eunuchs*, to add to the variety of their gross and unnatural pleasures ; while so extensive was the abuse of divorce, that even eight husbands+ in five years were insufficient to satisfy their insatiate desires.

These enormous vices, which Juvenal‡ has exposed with all the fire of his malignant genius, and occasionally arraigned with all the dignity of a true censor, seem to have reached their meridian at the period that Septimus Severus obtained the undisputed possession of the empire; for we find the laws then more disposed to throw a veil over the crimes of Rome, such

---

* Sunt quas eunuchi imbelles, ac mollia semper
   Oscula delectent, et desperatio barbæ
   Et quod abortivo non est opus.   *Sat. vi. v.* 365—367.

\+ Such at that time was the licence of divorce, that the above-mentioned number of husbands was permitted by the Roman law : and the epigrammatist, Martial, the contemporary of Juvenal, points his satire against Thelesina, as an adulteress, by representing her preposterous violation of the law, in having ten husbands in a month :—

   Aut minus, aut certe non plus tricessima lux est,
   Et nubit decimo, jam Thelesina viro.
   Quæ nubit toties, adultera lege est.   *Lib. vi. Epig. vii.*

‡ Whoever wishes to see an admirable picture of female licentiousness, drawn by the hand of a great master, should peruse the Tenth Satire of Juvenal.

was their nature and number, than to punish them. That successful and despotic Emperor was obliged to renounce his project of reformation, in consequence of finding three thousand accusations of adultery inscribed on the public register*.

But that this Essay may not be considered either as a satire or a panegyric upon the female character, instead of a collection of facts, we shall observe, that profligate as the age of Juvenal unquestionably was, yet the corruption was not so general, but some marks of ancient virtue could be traced. The poet, if the temper of his mind had led him to praise rather than to condemn, to exalt rather than to vilify, might have worthily commemorated the conjugal heroism of that Arria, who, to encourage her husband in his design of freeing himself from the vengeance of Claudius by death, first plunged the dagger in her own breast, and then presented it to him†. The same example

* Constantine was the first Roman Emperor who made a law to punish adultery with death.—*See Gothofred ad Cod. Theod. Lib. xi. Tit. xxxvi. p. 295.*

† This affecting incident is thus noticed in an epigram of Martial:—

> Casta suo gladium cum traderet Arria Pæto,
> Quem de visceribus traxerat ipsa suis;
> Si qua fides, vulnus quod feci, non dolet, inquit,
> Sed quod tu facies hoc mihi, Pæte, dolet.

Lib. i. Epis. xiv.

was followed by her daughter, the wife of Thrasea, and by the daughter of Thrasea, the wife of Helvidius Priscus, who both merited two such illustrious characters for their husbands. In handing down to execration the memory of Nero, Juvenal might have sung the praises of Paulina, the wife of Seneca, whose determination to share the same fate with her husband, was only prevented by the cruel kindness of Nero, and who exhibited in her countenance an honourable paleness*, which attested that part of her blood had flowed with that of her husband. A fit subject, also, for his independent muse, would have been the character of Agrippina, the wife of the celebrated Germanicus. Early doomed to experience the sad vicissitudes of fortune, a model of purity in the most vicious of periods, as implacable in her hatred of Tiberius, as faithful to her husband, she passed her life in lamenting the untimely fate of the one, and detesting the crimes of the other; and, as the satirist never lost an opportunity of exposing the inhumanity of the masters of the world, his energetic lines might have set before our eyes a most impressive picture of the

* Cui addidit paucos postea annos, laudabili in maritum memoria, *et ore ac manibus in eum pallorem albentibus, ut ostentui esset, multum vitalis spiritûs egestum.*—Tacitus Annalia, Lib. xv. Cap. lxiv.

unfeeling heart of Vespasian, which could not be moved even by the rare and unmerited sufferings of the virtuous Eponina. To escape the deadly hatred of the Emperor, her husband, Julius Sabinus, for nine successive years became the inhabitant of a subterraneous cavern. She found out his place of concealment, devoted her whole time to him, and sought to supply him with every comfort that could be enjoyed without liberty : they were, however, at last discovered. Incapable of being excited to compassion by the earnest intercessions of their friends, or by the more affecting sight of the innocent twins, the fruit of Eponina's visits to the cave, the brutish Vespasian sentenced the husband not to a simple and speedy, but to a cruel death. Torn from the embrace of her lord, the distracted wife, in the height of her resentment and despair, loaded the tyrant with reproaches, and exclaimed, in the presence of him, and of his courtiers, that she had lived more happily in the bowels of the earth, than he did, though surrounded by the splendor of a throne. This speech sealed her doom. But though neither her unhappy lot*, nor that of

* The romantic history of this affectionate couple, has been recorded by Plutarch, in his Amatoriæ Narrationes, p. 770, 771 : and two interesting tragedies in the French and Italian languages have been likewise

Arria and Agrippina, have arrested the notice of Juvenal, yet have their names been rescued from oblivion, and their virtues perpetuated in the immortal writings of Pliny and Tacitus.

In the commencement of the fourth century*, the introduction and establishment of the Christian religion into the Roman world, was the cause of another great revolution in the female character. The pagan theology was but ill-suited to improve the manners of women; for it partook more of ceremonies, than of precepts. Lustrations and processions supplied the place of a clear conscience, and an uniform course of virtue. It is easy, therefore, to conceive the mighty change which Christianity effected in them; since, among the severe laws which it imposed on women, it made marriage no longer a political, but a sacred tie; and did not confine its empire to their actions, but extended it even to their thoughts.

The legislation of the Greeks and Romans looked

founded upon it :—Sabine et Epponine Tragedie, par M. Richer.—Paris, Prault, 1735. Epponina, Tragedia di Ginseppe Bartoli in Torrino. Mairresse, 1767.

* In Anno Domini 324, circular letters were written by the orders of the Emperor to all his subjects, exhorting them to embrace the Christian religion, after his example.—*See Eusebius, Vita Constantini Magni, Lib. ii. Cap. xxiv—xlii, Cap. xlviii—lx.*

only to the political interest of societies; but the Christian code, while it inculcated the practice of every public and private virtue, inspired its followers with a contempt for this world, and sought to fix their minds upon a future state of rewards and punishments. This contempt of the world rendered them ambitious of perfection in the virtues of self-mortification and chastity. ' The life of woman, then, was one perpetual struggle between her sensual and her spiritual desires. To love and to cherish our fellow-creatures, was justly reckoned among the first of evangelical virtues. Women, young, rich, and beautiful, were in that age seen to abandon the amusements of the theatre, in order to comfort and relieve the aged, the sick, and the poor. The works of that successful advocate for celibacy, St. Jerom, perpetually resound with the praises of Paula*, her daughter Eustochium, and other illustrious penitents, who, by his eloquent persuasions, devoted their whole days and nights to the study of the scriptural writings.

When the Roman empire was overturned by the warlike barbarians of Scythia and Germany, to soften

---

* St. Jerom wrote a particular treatise upon the unexampled piety of that celebrated widow. It is to be found in his works, under the title of Epitaph. Paulæ.

their savage manners, Christianity passed from the vanquished to the conquerors, and was almost uniformly introduced by the female sex. It has been often remarked, that women have in all times been more possessed than men, with that ardent zeal for religion, which makes proselytism its chief aim; but to whatever cause this fact may be attributed, whether to their superior susceptibility of impression, or to their habits of quick and intelligent observation, it is indisputable, that most nations are indebted for their conversion to the charms of a believing queen. By such means, the evangelical light was gradually diffused through France, England, part of Germany, Bavaria, Hungary, Bohemia, Lithuania, Poland, and Russia: and, likewise, through female influence, Lombardy and Spain were led to renounce the doctrines of Arius.

In contemplating the invasion of the barbarians of the north, we cannot fail to be struck with the important changes which they introduced in manners: whoever studies their history, will perceive the invariable respect which they testified towards the female sex: their ferocity, as hunters or warriors, was softened only by the enthusiasm of love: their forests might be styled the cradles of chivalry*. To possess the object of his passion, the warrior was disposed to encounter every danger : frequently, a battle then could be viewed only as a number of separate duels, between combatants animated by a strong personal animosity against each other, in consequence of their ambition to signalize themselves in the eyes of their respective mistresses. From this cause, their native forests were oftentimes stained with blood, and the sword decided marriages as inheritances.

But though the barbarians, who overwhelmed the Roman world, had established a new system of manners and government, in the kingdoms they erected upon the ruins of that mighty empire, which gradually prepared the way for the reign of chivalry, yet many ages elapsed before it was considered as a political and military institution by the nations of Europe. The true spirit of chivalry did not begin to manifest itself until the middle or close of the eleventh century; yet the universal anarchy and discord, which had prevailed from the seventh century to that æra among the different states of Europe, (with the sole exception of

---

* Some faint vestiges of the ceremony of knighthood may be discovered in the early history of the Germans.—Framea scutoque juvenem ornant, says Tacitus, Germania, Cap. xiii.

those short, but splendid periods, in which a Charlemagne* and an Alfred appeared,) were even then far from having subsided. An almost perpetual shock was occasioned in manners, by christianity being mixed with the ceremonies of the ancient heathens; in polity and laws, by the rights of the priesthood being mixed with those of the throne; in government, by the prerogatives of kings being mixed with those of the nobility; and in religion, by the Arabians and Christians being mixed in Europe. From such contrasts flowed the sources of disorder and confusion; pilgrimages and massacres then oftentimes succeeded each other.

At the expiration, however, of the eleventh century, Europe, for the first time, saw all the nobles, who were inspired with a sentiment of equity, religion, and heroism, forming themselves into associations, to check the spirit of ferocity and violence. Their chief object was to take up arms against the Moors in Spain, the Saracens in the east, the tyrants of castles in Germany and France, to protect and avenge the innocent, the helpless, and the distressed; and,

* See the Reign of Charlemagne, considered chiefly with reference to Religion, Laws, Literature, and Manners.

above all, to defend the honour and rights of the fair sex, against the violence and oppression which they so often experienced.

Soon the spirit of a noble gallantry mingled itself in this memorable institution : each knight, in dedicating himself to the accomplishment of perilous adventures, established it as a point of honour to regard women in the light of sovereigns : to be insensible, indeed, to the passion of love, would have incapacitated the knight from discharging some of the most essential duties of his profession; and for her who was selected as the object of adoration, he attacked and defended, he stormed castles or cities, and gloried in shedding his own blood as much as that of his enemies. Decorated in his person with tokens of regard from the hand of his fair mistress, the knight roamed from court to court, from castle to castle, in search of opportunities to display his military virtues; for until he achieved some gallant exploit, either at home or abroad, a lady would have been irretrievably ruined, in the eyes of her kindred, had she turned a willing ear to the declaration of his attachment. The liberal sentiments therefore, and generous manners which chivalry introduced, and the marvellous respect and veneration it inculcated for the feebler sex, may be said to

have laid the foundation of a system, which first required that women should be addressed in a style of
gentleness, delicacy, and attention, unknown to the
Greeks and Romans in their most polished periods,
and which gave them that sensibility and refinement,
that influence and consideration in society, by which
they are now distinguished.

Let us stop, then, for a moment, to throw a rapid
glance upon the revolution produced in the condition
and manners of women, by the genius of chivalry:
subject before to every species of neglect and ill usage,
from the rudeness and brutality of man, it was one of
the effects of this singular institution, to set them up
to be worshipped as idols by their slaves or servants,
the respectful titles assumed by their admirers. Love
was inseparable from honour: the ladies, proud of
their empire, shared the noble passions which they inspired. Inaccessible to every sentiment unallied with
glory, their manners were at once dignified, heroic,
and tender. The female, who so far lost sight of the
established maxims of the age, as to forget to reverence
the chastity of her own person, was sure to encounter
universal contempt and insult; while such was the
homage paid to those whose virtue was unsullied, that
the slightest mark of disrespect shewn to them by an

uncourteous knight, exposed him to the danger and infamy of being treated as a common enemy, by all who were mindful of the oath which they had taken to become the champion of God and the ladies*.

Such was the rank and dignity which the spirit of chivalry imparted to the female sex, and such the fine propriety and guarded sensibility it rigidly exacted from them. It gave birth, also, to an innumerable multitude of works in praise of women. The verses of the bards, better known by the name of Trouverres, or Troubadours, the Italian sonnet, the plaintive romance, the poems of chivalry, and the Spanish and French romances, may be regarded as so many monuments descriptive of the love and gallantry of the times. In every rehearsal of mimic war, in tilts, tournaments, and battles, all bore a strong relation to women. The same propensity to magnify and exalt the female character, manifested itself in the lively writings of those days. The warrior and poet were then characters analogous to each other. The hand

* The most ample information relative to the rights and privileges of the order of chivalry, and the various important duties it imposed on those who were admitted into it, may be collected in Memoirs sur l'Ancienne Chivalrie consideree comme une Etablissement Politique et Militaire, par M. de la Curne de St. Palaye.

which brandished the lance, also touched the lyre, in honour of the sovereign of his affections.

That romantic spirit of bravery which oftentimes prompted the candidate for knighthood to attempt impossibilities, was communicated, in a great measure, to women : the crusades furnish us with many examples of their enthusiastic zeal and courage. In the field of battle they have remained firm and undismayed ; and, animated by the double force of religion and valour, have died with arms in their hands, by the sides of their lovers or husbands. In Europe, the attack or defence of a pass, or castle, was oftentimes undertaken by women; and princesses then commanded armies, and gained victories*. Such, among many others, was the celebrated Jane of Flanders, Countess of Mountfort, who protected Brittany against the united attacks of the French, Spaniards, and Genoese, by an example of female skill and valour that has not been surpassed in any age or country.

The next revolution which took place in the female character, may be attributed to the revival of letters in

* Those times would seem to render Plato's notion of assigning the same employments to women as to men, of committing to them the command of armies, and the government of states, not quite so great a paradox as it has been generally considered.

Italy. Before that memorable epoch, the thick darkness of ignorance was spread over Europe; but when the minds of men were supplied with proper models and materials, they began gradually to recover their powers. Women, too, were likewise ambitious of shewing that their mental faculties were not inferior to those of the other sex. Alessandra, the daughter of Bartolomeo Scala, chancellor of the republic of Florence, is said to have been equally conversant with the Greek and Latin tongues, at a very early age; and some of her verses, in the former language, are to be found in the works of that celebrated scholar Politian; while the famous Cassandra Fideles, of Venice, may be justly regarded as a prodigy of classical literature. Such, indeed, were her extraordinary acquirements, that her name deservedly holds a high rank, even among the learned of Italy*.

So strong, at that period, was the passion of women for letters, and so great their proficiency in them, that we even find some desirous of exhibiting the fruits of their studies to a public audience. In the fourteenth cen-

---

* Her letters and orations were published at Pavia, in 1636, by Jac. Philip Thomassini, a bishop in the republic of Venice. For a more particular account of this learned lady, and likewise of Alessandra, I must refer the reader to Mr. Roscoe's justly celebrated Life of Lorenzo de Medici, Octavo Edit. *vol. II. p.* 130, 134.

tury, the daughter of a gentleman of Bologna devoted herself to the study of the Latin language and jurisprudence: at the age of three and twenty she pronounced a funeral oration in Latin, in the great church of Bologna; and, three years after, she took the degree of Doctor, and publicly read the Institutes of Justinian, in her native city. When she had completed her thirtieth year, her reputation was so great as to raise her to the chair of jurisprudence; and her lectures were frequented by a crowd of disciples, composed of various countries and ages. The picture of this extraordinary female will be heightened by adding that, with these more masculine endowments, she possessed all the charms and beauty of her own sex*.

At the end of the fourteenth century, when the knowledge of the Greek, as well as the Latin tongue, was spread over Italy, the merits of Aristotle and

---

* M. Thomas, in his admirable Essai sur le Caractere, les Mœurs, et l'Esprit des Femmes dans les differents Siecles, *p.* 86, to which I am indebted for many of the conclusions drawn from the facts related in this discourse, tells us, that in the fourteenth and fifteenth centuries, the same prodigy was renewed in the same city ; and it is worthy of remark, that, in the eighteenth century, a female was again raised to a chair at Bologna : it was the celebrated Laura Bassi who obtained this distinction. Her letters upon natural philosophy are said to have first instigated her relative, Lazarus Spallanzani, to the pursuit of a science, in which he afterwards acquired such high renown.

Plato divided the attention of the learned : the church and universities paid a servile respect and veneration to the dogmatic opinions of the former*, while the writings of the latter philosopher were universally admired by poets, lovers, and women. The study of classic literature was not, however, destined to be confined to Italy : the rest of Europe was soon animated with a similar spirit. The fifteenth and sixteenth centuries saw France, Spain, Germany, and England, introduced to an acquaintance with the poets, philosophers, orators, and historians, of Greece and Rome ; and the records of those times bear ample testimony, that women were so distinguished for their learning, as to be qualified to enter the lists with men in literary contests ;. to sustain Theses in public assemblies ; to preach and mix in controversies ; to fill the chair of philosophy and jurisprudence ; to harangue

* About that period he began to obtain the title of *Philosopher*, by way of pre-eminence : and his authority in philosophy (such an object was he of excessive admiration, observes Bacon,) was equal to that of St. Paul in divinity. *See Bacon, Opus Majus, edit. a Jebb, p.* 36. To such a remarkable pitch was this veneration for Aristotle then carried, that in some of the most renowned universities, especially in that of Paris, the students were obliged to take a solemn oath to defend the opinions of Aristotle, of his commentator Averrois, and of his other ancient commentators.—*See Bulæi, Hist. Univer. Parisien, Tom, IV. p.* 275.

in Latin before Popes; to write Greek; and to study Hebrew*.

Women then dedicated themselves to the pursuit of learning with an ardour and devotion, of which it is difficult to form any idea in these times: this passion was alike felt in cloisters, courts, and even upon thrones. In the times of which we are speaking, one of the chief objects in the minds of English queens was, the acquisition of the ancient languages. Catharine Parr is said to have translated a book; and Lady Jane Grey's fame as a scholar†, if we look to the age in which she lived, cannot be too highly extolled, or too loudly applauded. It is well known, that Elizabeth was intimately acquainted with the Greek and Latin classics, nor was her knowledge of the French and Spanish

* M. Thomas, in his Essay before referred to, pages 87—91, has given us the names of those females who have rendered themselves eminent in different countries, either by their own writings, or by their indefatigable application to the study of the ancient languages.

† The letter she addressed to her sister, in the Greek language, the night before her execution, the purport of which was to exhort her " to live and die in the true christian faith," may be cited as an equal proof of her uncommon proficiency in classical learning, and her presence of mind upon that trying occasion. It is to be found in Heylin's History of the Reformation of the Church of England, *p.* 166, 167.

languages less profound*; while, from the following sentence of an author who lived and wrote in her reign, it would appear, that the ladies of the court had imitated her example:—" The stranger†," says Harrison, " that entereth the Court of England, upon the sudden, shall rather imagine himself come into some public school of the University, where many give ear to one that readeth unto them, than into a prince's palace, if you confer this with those of other nations." The hours now bestowed at the glass and the toilet, were then passed in studying the writings of the ancients.

Many pens were employed in commemorating the praises of illustrious women : Italy began soon to be overwhelmed with works of this description. After Boccacio's Panegyric de Claris Mulieribus, upwards of twenty writers published successively eulogies upon the celebrated women of all nations. About the end

* The famous Roger Ascham, in proclaiming the scholastic attainments of his royal pupil Elizabeth, observes, to use his own words, " Yea, I believe, that besides her perfect readiness in Latin, Italian, French, and Spanish, she readeth here now at Windsor, more Greek every day, than some prebendary of this church doth Latin in a whole week." See the Schoolmaster.

† See Description of Britain, Book ii. Chap. xv. This work was printed in 1577.

of the fourteenth century, Brantome produced his entertaining work, *Memoires des Dames Illustres.* It has the unpardonable fault, however, of substituting too often adulation in the place of truth. Even the characters of Jane of Naples, and of Catharine de' Medici, this complacent biographer can consider as fit subjects for unbounded panegyric; although the first has been accused, by the impartiality of all contemporary historians, as the murderer of her husband; and the second as the author of the civil wars in France, and the chief promoter of the massacre of the Huguenots: yet does not Brantome scruple, in his excessive admiration of the fair sex, to maintain them innocent of those flagitious acts.

The next commendatory work upon the female sex came from the pen of Hilarion de Coste. His ponderous volumes contained the eulogies of all the women in the fifteenth or sixteenth century, who were either distinguished by their courage, their talents, or their virtues: but we must not expect a bigoted catholic to be much inclined to break forth into a strain of compliment upon those who were not attached to his theological tenets. Accordingly we find, that Hilarion de Coste passes over in total silence the name of Queen Elizabeth, and indulges himself in a long and pompous eulogium upon the merits of her predecessor, who commenced her reign by the murder of the most accomplished of women, Lady Jane Grey; and who has deservedly incurred the execration of posterity, for having brought, in the short space of five years*, two hundred and seventy-seven persons to the stake, on account of religion.

The same spirit which produced in those times so many panegyrics upon illustrious women, prepared the way for almost an equal number of publications upon the merits of women in general. The pre-eminence of the sex (to such a pinnacle of perfection was the female character then supposed to have attained) began, for the first time, to be proposed as a question for public debate. Among those who peculiarly signalized themselves as the assertors of the superiority of women, was that extraordinary man, Cornelius Agrippa. His history is so singular, as to merit particular notice. He was born at Cologne, in 1486, and deduced his origin from a noble family. At an early age he entered into the service of the Emperor Maxi-

---

* The period that Mary reigned; and it is computed that, in that time, five bishops, twenty-one clergymen, eight lay gentlemen, eighty-four artificers, one hundred husbandmen and labourers, fifty-five women, and four children, were burnt.—*See Heylin's History of the Reformation, p.* 252.

milian, and obtained from him the post of secretary: but the sword being as familiar to him as the pen, he sought fame and military experience for seven years, in the army of Italy, and, as a recompence for his exploits, received the honor of knighthood. He aspired also to academical as well as to martial honors, and took the different degrees of Doctor of Divinity, Laws, and Medicine, with great eclat. He was master of eight languages; and such was the versatility of his genius, and such the equal activity of his body and mind, that he commented upon the Epistles of St. Paul, in England; gave lectures upon the philosopher's stone, at Turin; taught theology at Pavia; and practised medicine in Switzerland. His eminent talents were engaged successively in the service of three or four princes and princesses; but his lofty and captious temper rendered him alike incapable of submitting to slavery, or enjoying freedom. Considered as a magician by the superstition of his times, a proficient in most sciences, and twice imprisoned for the boldness of his writings, he finished his career in France, in the forty-ninth year of his age, after having excited the pity, admiration, and contempt, of the learned of Europe*.

* For a full account of his adventurous life, see Bayle's Dictionaire Historique et Critique.

It was in 1509, that Cornelius Agrippa published his famous treatise, *De Fœminei Sexus Præcellentiâ.* From the circumstance, however, of his being at that time a dependant upon the bounty of the famous Margaret of Austria, who governed the Low Countries, his enemies have not been wanting to insinuate, that interest, more than inclination, directed his pen upon this occasion. It must be confessed, at the first glance, that the nature of his connection with that princess, might seem to authorize such an opinion; but whoever has perused the work in question, cannot fail to acknowledge, that the author of it writes like one who is completely enamoured of his subject. No doating lover ever ransacked his brains more for similes to illustrate the superlative beauty and accomplishments of his mistress, than Cornelius Agrippa has done to exalt the female above the male sex. His book is divided into thirty chapters; and in each chapter he attempts to demonstrate the superiority of women, from proofs theological, physical, historical, cabalistical, and moral. Fable, poetry, and history, laws civil and canonical, are jumbled together, in strange confusion, to support the cause which he so heartily espoused; and his singular discourse (in which a great display of learning is certainly exhibited) is concluded by the solemn assurance, that not interest, but duty, is the real motive which has prompted him to undertake it; since, to know a truth, and not to proclaim it, is to be regarded, according to his judgment, in the light of a criminal silence.

But though the merits of this performance are not of the first rate, it is still entitled to notice, as an authentic indication of the unbounded respect and admiration then shewn to the female sex*. The sixteenth century may be perhaps viewed as the most brilliant epoch for women: after this period, the number of pieces in prose and poetry in their praises considerably diminished ; the final extinction of chivalry in Europe, the abolition of tournaments, the wars of religion in Germany, France, and England, and the new taste of society, which, by increasing the intercourse of the sexes, corrupted their morals, may be referred to as the principal causes for the abatement of that, we had almost said, unnatural refinement, which required from the lover the most distant and respectful homage to the object of his passion, and, on her part, a reserve and chastity which bordered

---

* The opinion of Aristotle in his Poetics, *cap. xv.* "*That it is probable a woman should be worse than a man,*" would have found but few supporters in that age.

oftentimes upon a ludicrous absurdity*. Still, however, beauty, as a possession, was perhaps then more coveted than by the heroes of chivalry; nor was that romantic spirit of gallantry less frequent, which instigates the lover to the most daring efforts of valour, for the sole purpose of obtaining the admiration of the fair mistress of his affections: but, after all, the only essential difference between the two systems may be said to consist, in the first regarding sensual pleasure as a secondary, and the latter as a primary object.

If we take a view of the state of women in the seventeenth century, it will be found, that while a free communication between the sexes was only gradually commencing in Germany, England, and Spain, it was then carried to the highest pitch in Italy and France: in the latter country especially, women of high birth began to abandon all taste for severe studies, and to confine themselves to the acquirement of those accomplishments which might heighten the effect of their personal charms; then did they display for the first time that exquisite grace in their manners, that unaffected freedom and elegance of conversation, which have ever since so peculiarly distinguished them to

* Various and curious instances are given by M. de la Curne de St. Palaye, in his Memoires sur l'Ancienne Chevalerie, &c. &c.

their advantage, from the rest of their sex in Europe.; and such is the striking inconsistency of human conduct and human affairs, that the period when the women of France became as it were *the glass of fashion* to those of other European nations, was apparently the most unlikely one for such a circumstance;—when their own country was exposed to all the horrors of civil anarchy and bloodshed!

Under the regency of Anne of Austria, the women of France acquired that dominion over the minds of their husbands and lovers, which they seem to have preserved, with very little diminution, down to the times in which we live. The famous Cardinal Retz, in his account of the Frondeurs, has fully shewn us, how entirely love presided over all their intrigues*. A revolution in the heart of a woman then often produced a revolution in the state of public affairs. Women, in the periods to which we allude, occasionally appeared at the head of factions; while their persons were decorated with scarfs, for the purpose of distinguishing the party to which they belonged. In the same saloon were seen instruments of war mixed with instruments of music; violins with cuirasses. Women, illustrious by their birth, and eminent for their beauty,

* See Memoires de Cardinal Retz.

oftentimes visited the troops, and appeared in the councils of war*.

In respect to the gallantry of those times, it is well known to have been of the most romantic kind. Possessed of the warm passions of a Spaniard, Anne of Austria herself is said, if we listen to the scandalous tales of the *Fronde*, to have frequently deviated from the line of virtue in the attachment she manifested to her favourites. To render a public homage to beauty, was considered an act of duty on the part of man. The most trifling occurrences were classed with things of importance, if women were at all concerned in them. The gift of a bracelet or glove was esteemed an event in a man's life; and love or gallantry was deemed as fit a subject for serious discussion, as the loss or gain of a battle. In two lines, less remarkable for their poetry than for an extravagant hyperbole, the Duc de la Rochefoucault assures Madame de Longueville, that, to merit her affections, he had made war against kings, and would against the gods themselves†.

---

* There was a regiment created under the name of *Mademoiselle;* and Monsieur wrote to the ladies who attended his daughter to Orleans, in the following manner:—" A Mesdames les Comtesses Maréchales de camp, dans l'armée de ma fille contre le Mazarin."

† Pour meriter son cœur, pour plaire a ses beaux yeux,
   J'ai fait la guerre aux Roix; je l'aurois fait aux Dieux.

The lover of the beautiful Mademoiselle de Guerchi, M. de Chatillon, wore her garter upon his arm in one battle; and we also read, in the memoirs of those times, that the Duc de Bellegarde, the distinguished favourite of the queen, on the eve of his departure to command an army, solicited her to honour him so far as to touch the hilt of his sword.

From that period to the present, it may be safely asserted, that in proportion to the advancement of the fine arts in the countries of Europe, have been the improvements in the state and accomplishments of women: they may now be said to have struck a deep root in that fairest and most enlightened portion of the globe. Even in Spain and Russia*, where the progress of the arts has been so slow, in comparison with other European countries, from the superstitious and tyrannical spirit of those governments, the women are now beginning to mix in society, and consequently to act on the same principles of equality, independence and freedom, as those in France and England.

Having now contemplated women in different epochs and countries, it only remains for us to speak

---

* See the reign of Peter the Great, in the Revolutions of Russia, 2d edit. for the low state of the arts in the seventeenth and eighteenth centuries.

of their actual condition and character ; but that we may not needlessly lengthen an essay already too long, we shall confine our observations to those of our own country.

Whoever surveys the condition of woman in savage and civilized life, will perceive, that in the one and the other she may be said to touch the extremes of misery and happiness. Of the benefits then which result from an age of high refinement, like the present, there can be no question but that women receive their full share. Without regarding them like the sons of chivalry or romance, as beings of a superior order, we yet acknowledge in every act the influence which they possess over our society. We in fact consider them as the grand spring which puts it in motion. Capable of imparting whatever form they please to society, it must be a matter of great satisfaction to every thinking mind, to perceive that this influence on the part of women is properly exerted ; for it will not be denied, even by those who are disposed to entertain the most gloomy apprehensions respecting the future destiny of Britain, that the female character never stood higher for the cultivation of private virtue of every kind than in the present times.

In spite of the general licentiousness which reigns

on the Continent, softness, delicacy, and purity, are still the characteristics of the females of this island. They have not learned as yet to mistake effrontery for dignity; and they still consider, that the most indispensable of all their virtues, and that by which they obtain the greatest influence over our sex, is modesty. The absence, indeed, of this virtue, excludes all the rest, which are its inseparable concomitants; and such is the inexpressibly captivating effect of it over their whole character, that it is the observation of Madame de Sevigné, whose acquaintance with human nature, and skill in the portraiture of every feminine passion, was inferior to none, that women should preserve their modesty, even in the very moment they are going to part with it.

The intellectual powers of our fair countrywomen are now beginning to take a wider range than they have hitherto done. Few subjects can be presented, upon which their extensive reading does not enable them to throw out some suitable ideas. In the days of the Spectator, the greater part of the fine ladies conducted themselves as if they had really adopted that tenet of Mahomet, which forbade all kind of study to their sex: their shameful privilege of doing nothing was then claimed and made use of to the fullest extent;

whereas, the most dissipated votaries of fashion, we believe, can now find time to cultivate their minds, while some individuals in the female community exhibit talents of the very first order. Abundant proofs, indeed, will be found in the records of authentic history, to justify the assertion, that genius has no sex. In all the departments of literature, except the philosophical, women, we profess to think, have nearly reached to an equal degree of excellence with men ; and in some, we will venture to add, eclipsed them.

We are not, however, ignorant, that the celebrated Descartes has boasted of the philosophical spirit of women ; but the impartial examiner of his life will not fail to recollect, that at the time he committed this error, (in our judgment,) he was persecuted by envy, and chiefly admired by two princesses. Possible it is, too, that in his royal pupils, Elizabeth and Christina, he found clearness, order, and method ; but the foundation of the philosophical spirit, that hesitation and cold reason which measures every step it takes, we suspect were not to be traced in their understandings. The female mind is quick and penetrating ; but to investigate a subject in all its relations, is a task which it is almost incapable of performing : it has more sallies* than efforts. That patient induction, therefore, which leads to the discovery of great and important truths, cannot be looked for in the intellectual character of the softer sex: but though we are not disposed to admit, that the mind of woman, in the foregoing respect, is endowed with the same powers as that of man, justice requires us to remember, that Madame de Chatelet made such proficiency in the study of abstracted sciences and difficult researches, as to illustrate Leibnitz, and to translate and comment upon Newton†.

In the eye of the moralist, luxury is conceived to be peculiarly ruinous to the female character. To every true lover of his country it cannot then but be a source of high consolation to observe, that in the present period of excessive refinement and corruption, the religious, domestic, and social virtues, instead of being abjured by women, as some writers would plainly wish to insinuate, are more strictly fulfilled by them

---

* Women, says a very sagacious observer of the female character, have most wit, men most genius; women observe, men reason.—*See Rousseau's Emilius.*

† Gaëtasia Agnesia produced likewise two profound and excellent volumes on Mathematics.—*See British Critic, vol. XXIII, p.* 143, *XXIV,* 653—*and XXV,* 141.

than by our sex. The spectacle is now by no means rare, of the father and sons of a family being familiar with all the immoralities of fashionable life, while the mother and daughters are remarkable for the piety of their sentiments, and the purity of their conduct. Nor can these religious impressions be ascribed to the consequence of leading a secluded and contemplative life; since the modern system of manners gives to the females the most unbounded liberty. In the social virtues, too, it does not appear to us by any means extravagant to think, that the women of the present age are infinitely more conversant than our sex. If we judge women after nature, and judge them after society, especially the society of great cities, it will perhaps be found, that in the latter state, the general desire of pleasing stifles, in a great measure, all those sweet and affectionate passions which are comprized under the virtues of sensibility: nevertheless, though they are continually exposed, in their intercourse with the world, to meet with rivals in rank, beauty, fortune, and intellect—circumstances which are somewhat apt to freeze their more amiable feelings, and to discourage the reciprocation of social kindnesses,— still we are inclined to believe, that their constancy in friendship and love is more durable than that of men.

In that species of heroic friendship, which shrinks from no sacrifice nor danger to support the object of our regard, the women are, from the delicacy of their character, perhaps inferior to men: in other respects, the female disposition is better adapted to the cultivation of friendship. Our rough, unbending, and unaccommodating nature, is little indeed framed to display those delicate and tender sentiments which may be said to constitute the graces of friendship. Oftentimes we wound most when we attempt to administer comfort; and, unlike the fair sex, in estimating the perfections and imperfections of our friends, we are more disposed to dwell upon their failings than their virtues.

> At nos virtutes ipsas invertimus, atque
> Sincerum cupimus vas incrustare.
>
> *Horace, Lib. i. Sat. iii.*

In great occasions, then, the friendship of the man perhaps is to be preferred; but for our ordinary happiness, we cannot help thinking, that female friendship is most to be desired.

With respect to the attachments of the heart, the rapidity with which they shoot forth, and die away, among our own sex, would plainly seem to indicate, that in unshaken constancy the women are superior to the men. We might, indeed, be rather led to expect, from the excessive adulation which is so universally offered to them, (for they, like princes, seldom hear the truth,) that their capriciousness would have been proverbial: the number of victims to male inconstancy and perjury, prove it however to be otherwise. May not this superior durability of affection in the female character, be accounted for, from the circumstance of our sex being destined either to active or public life, the busy scenes of which rarely permit them to make love the ruling passion of their souls; whereas, from the exemption of women from all public employments, their mind, heart, imagination, and memory, are all affected by it, and it becomes the most important concern of their life?

We are perfectly aware of the numerous exceptions to these remarks, in the present age; that there are many women in the middling and higher classes of society, who set no value upon accomplishments which adorn retirement; whose mornings are spent in coquetry, and nights in gaming; who talk of marriage as if treachery and infidelity were its inseparable concomitants; who practice every kind of vice and folly in succession; and whose last groan, we may say with St. Evremond, is more for the loss of their beauty than their life. Yet we may confidently boast, that the majority of the female sex, in this happy island, cultivate literature, and esteem it for its own sake, and not for a vain and frivolous reputation; and keep their esteem for virtue, their contempt for vice, their sensibility for friendship, and their affection entire for their families, uncontaminated by all such disgraceful examples.

ESSAY V.

ON THE FORMATION OF NATIONAL CHARACTERS FROM PHYSICAL CAUSES.

AMONG philosophical and speculative men, few subjects have been thought more worthy of examination than that one, of how far the climates of different countries affect their forms of government. Those theories, which ascribe the habits of government entirely to the influences of climate and situation, appear to us as absurd and extravagant as any which can be traced in the Republic of Plato, or the Utopia of Sir Thomas More. We shall, therefore, content ourselves with taking a summary view of them, without entering into a refutation of the radically erroneous reasonings of those who deny the operation altogether of moral causes upon the spirit and intelligence of the great mass of a nation.

That the northern inhabitants of the globe are more inclined to laborious exertions than those who are exposed to the vertical rays of the sun, is a position which appears undeniable to us; but where the air is most temperate, and the soil rich and inviting, that there we should certainly find a lively fancy and ardour of soul, the fairest shoots of eloquence, and an extreme delicacy of taste, is a conclusion which we are not warranted to make, either from a past or present view of the history of mankind: nor can it be laid down as a principle, without very considerable modification, that undaunted resolution, and the most solid improvement in the study of science, are to be regarded as the peculiar properties of the inhabitants of a cold region.

It must be obvious to every one, that excessive heat is not calculated to render the body patient of fatigue. In the torrid zone, where the fruits of the earth spring up almost spontaneously, the disposition to sloth may be indulged without any danger of wanting the necessaries of life: on the contrary, those who dwell in cold countries must labour, or else be exposed to the miseries of famine. In this manner, we can account for the southern Asiatic displaying, in general, less vigour and strength of body than the northern European. It is however asserted, by Montesquieu and other philosophers, that the qualities of the air and climate affect, in a powerful degree, the conduct and characters of nations. According to them, we are to believe, that great heat, by relaxing the fibres, and by extending the surface of the skin where the action of the nerves is chiefly performed, excites an uncommon sensibility to all external subjects; consequently, an exquisite imagination, taste, sensibility, and vivacity, are to be peculiar to those latitudes where the fig and the vine, the tamarind and the pine-apple, grow in the greatest natural perfection; while those, on the other hand, who live in cold climates, are said to acquire a cast of mind and temper of an opposite complexion.

But to us, no position seems more deficient in solidity than that, *Ingenia* hominum ubique locorum *situs* format*. We profess to think, that the intellectual operations of the mind are no more dependant upon the difference of heat and cold, of moisture or dryness, than that ferocity and cruelty are the necessary consequences of devouring a large quantity of animal food†: for, entertaining the opinion that genius, in

* See Quintus Curtius, Lib. viii. cap. ix.

† " Il est certain," says Rousseau, " que les grands mangeurs de viande sont en general cruels et feroces plus que les autres hommes. Cette observation est de tous les lieux, et de touts les tems. La barbare Angloise est connue." *See Emile, Tom. I. p.* 274. But the unsubstantial diet which the French are famed for using, has produced effects, unfortunately, too well calculated to refute the justness of that obser-

all its multifarious forms, is the product of every country, the following reasons, we conceive, may be satisfactorily urged.

If it be true, that the qualities of air and soil usurp a decided influence over the temperament and understanding of a people, it will necessarily follow, that those people, whose situation with respect to climate is similar, should be found counterparts to each other in their manners, dispositions, or pursuits: but what resemblance, we should like to know, can be traced between the reserve and melancholy of the Dane, and the loquacity and sprightliness of the Swede, so justly styled the Frenchman of the north? And, in the contiguous governments of China and Japan, who will undertake to prove any similarity between the habits and principles of these two people? The distance from Athens to Sparta, or Thebes, was not so great, that many hours were consumed, even by lazy travellers, before they reached those places; yet, in spite of the intimate connection which existed, at

vation. Our countryman, Sir William Temple, in his account of the United Provinces, has fallen almost into the same error, by remarking, that all fierce and bold animals are carnivorous. *Vol. I. p.* 166.—But Mr. Hume, in his admirable Essay upon National Characters, points out, with his usual acuteness, the Swedes, as a striking exception to this general observation. *Vol. I. p.* 210, different periods, between those several states, their national peculiarities were as striking as those of the English, the Welsh, the Scots, and the Irish. A dyke of twenty-four miles separates us from the French; the Englishman, however, who sets his foot in Calais, finds there as opposite a set of manners and usages from those of his own country, as if he had already reached the central province of France. If England, and the neighbouring country of France, present such an uniform spectacle of dissimilar manners, it would assuredly be the most paradoxical species of reasoning, to ascribe that contrast to the immediate operation of climate.

We are persuaded then that the great and striking diversity of manners between nations removed from each other, as France and England, must be attributed to the influences of moral causes, by which are chiefly understood the nature of the government, the freedom or slavery, the affluence or poverty, in which the people live; their disposition to warlike or pacific habits; their antipathy to the commercial, or attachment to the fine arts. The inhabitants of this country are alike famed, throughout Europe, for their commercial spirit and unbounded love of liberty; yet he would justly subject himself to the imputation of light-headiness, who should place those qualities to the effect of its climate, and not to the peculiar form of government, to which it has been accustomed for ages, and to which, though it may have been changed for a time, the nation has always reverted on the first opportunity. Montesquieu seems to us to have pushed his favourite theory, of the capability of the soil to infuse habits for government, to the very confines of absurdity, when he attributes our impatient disposition to the scurvy, and to the cast of our constitution, in which there is so much of the democratic mould, as to give us those notions of freedom and independence, that we become restless under any situation which imposes a restraint upon our desires.

In the minority of Louis the Fourteenth, the French parliament planned the following permanent law, which was in the nature of a Habeas Corpus Bill; namely, that every prisoner, in twenty-four hours after his confinement, should be examined by the parliament as to the purport of his crime; but, because this wise and humane proposition was but feebly supported, and in the end abandoned, by the ministry of that day, are we justified in concluding from thence, that the parliament was incapable from physical causes of adhering to any settled plan of liberty ? We should think, that no one who is conversant with the civil wars which raged when Anne of Austria held the French sceptre, would subscribe to such an opinion; as he must find abundant proofs in the history of that period* to satisfy him, that the temporizing and vacillating character shewn by the honest part of the parliament, was solely attributable to the despotism which then prevailed in their government, in spite of all the generous efforts which they had made to temper it with a mixture of aristocracy and republicanism.

The character, indeed, of a nation in an advanced period of civilization, may be said to depend almost entirely upon moral causes. The influence of government, for instance, upon manners and literature, cannot but be obvious to the most careless observer. Under the baneful sway of an arbitrary power, we look in vain for freedom of manners and conversation, even in the most indifferent circumstances of life. The bulk of the people must there conform to the court model; its will must be to them the only rule of right, or wrong; since he who ventures to deviate from it inevitably becomes the object of ministerial vengeance. A government of this description will shew as despotic

---

* See Memoires d' Anne d' Austriche, by Madame de Motteville, Tom. II.

a controul in matters poetical as political. When the jealous, irascible spirit of Cardinal Richelieu had revenged itself on Corneille, by compelling the French academy to censure his immortal production the *Cid*, instead of venturing to wage an open war with the Cardinal, the poet seems to have been overwhelmed with terror and confusion at his proceedings, as we may gather from the following passage in his letter to M. de Boisrobert, the minister's favourite;—" It is with the utmost impatience I look for the sentiments of the academy, to determine the course which I may henceforth pursue; since in the present interval I cannot labour with any confidence, and dare not hazard any word without trembling for my safety*."

It was the established practice in the governments of Spain and Portugal to prohibit the publication of any work, without its first having undergone six or seven official reviews. The superior genius of Cervantes, Lope de Vega, or Camoens, might burst through all such obstructions in their road to fame; yet it will assuredly not be contended, that in those countries

---

* J'attends avec beaucoup d'impatience les sentimens de l'Academie, afin d'apprendre ce que dorenavant je dois suivre. Jusques là, je ne puis travailler qù avec defiance, et ne s' employer un mot en sûreté.—*See P. Pelisson, Histoire de l'Academie Françoise.*

where the Inquisition is appointed the sovereign arbiter of the fate of all candidates for literary glory, the people will discover the state abuses, or be encouraged to redress them from the scope and tendency of their writings. As well, therefore, may we deny, that sadness and melancholy are not associated with solitude, joy and pleasure with society, as attribute the gloom and melancholy so observable among Spaniards to the influence of physical causes, and not to the tyrannic spirit of their municipal laws; or suppose that the decline of the frank and libertine wit of the old Roman comedy, was not chiefly owing to the studied and cautious manners which the artful policy of Augustus introduced, before he attempted to undermine the authority of the people.

From these several observations it will appear, that we profess to belong to that sect, if we may be allowed this expression, who are disposed to circumscribe the influence of physical causes upon the political constitution of states within very narrow limits. Man, in a state of barbarity, may be tutored in some degree by the elements; may be allowed perhaps to imbibe certain habits and dispositions from the air he breathes, and the food he takes; but when he emerges from the condition of a savage, and becomes familiarized to all

the comforts and refinements of civil society, the connection between genius and climate, we then suppose,
ceases, or is felt only in a very remote degree. If we
consult the page of historic truth, it will incontestibly
prove to us,

> " Summos posse viros, et magna exempla daturos,
> " Vervecum in patria ; crassoque sub aëre nasci ;"
>
> *Juvenal, Sat. x. Book xlix.*

and that the poets of the north may aspire to as conspicuous a place in the annals of fame as those of the
south. Dante, Tasso, Ariosto, and Petrarch, are the
pride and glory of the Italians ; but let him pronounce
who is capable of reading their works in the original,
and those of Shakespeare, Milton, Dryden, and Pope,
whether our countrymen are not entitled to a higher
tribute of admiration than their rivals, on the same
score of invention,—a faculty which unquestionably
holds the first place among the virtues of a poet. In
a word, the difference between an ignorant and an enlightened government cannot be more strikingly exemplified than in the energy and solicitude with which
the former operates upon the moral feelings of a people,
and in the supineness and negligence with which the
latter suffers the influence of mere natural causes to
decide upon the destinies and manners of a nation.

ESSAY VI.

ON THE RAPID GROWTH OF METHODISM.

WE have of late been in the habit of witnessing so many political convulsions, that those evils which do not instantly threaten to overwhelm us, excite no very lively sensations of alarm in our breasts,—else, before this time, a thousand orthodox pens would have filled every corner of the kingdom with relations of the various evils and dangers to which the church and state were equally exposed, from the amazing increase of Methodism ; a subject of so great and tremendous a nature, that, compared with it, that of the catholic emancipation shrinks into total insignificance.

Our curiosity then is naturally prompted to inquire by what means a religious sect, in an age, the characteristic of which is certainly not very favourable to the spirit of proselytism, should have made such rapid strides within the short space of sixty years, as to number among its disciples, secret and avowed, seven hundred thousand people, composed however chiefly of the low and middling classes of the community? The term Methodist we know, strictly speaking, can only be applied to the followers of Wesley* and Whitfield; but we have used it in a more extensive sense, and under that name designated all the *evangelical* dissenters who form, what has been emphatically called, " the combined armies against the church of England."

To this enquiry we shall studiously endeavour to bring a mind divested of all those prepossessions arising out of that reverence which we entertain for the consecrated servants of our faith; since it must be admitted with regret, that this most serious and important subject has been hitherto treated, with only one or two exceptions, in a tone too magisterial and virulent to confer the slightest service upon the interests of true religion. After a careful examination then into the various causes of the increase of Methodism, we are inclined to think that it has been chiefly promoted and diffused by the seven following:—1. The prejudices of the common people against episcopacy.—2. The

* A Fellow of Merton College first distinguished Mr. Wesley and his adherents by the appellation of Methodists, in allusion to an ancient college of physicians at Rome, who were remarkable for putting their patients under regimen, and were therefore called Methodists.—*See Cooke's Life of Wesley.*

Methodist doctrines of the immediate and perpetual interference of Providence, of experience, and justification by faith only.—3. Their class meetings.—4. Extemporaneous preaching.—5. Affected sanctity and austerity of manners.—6. The imperfect residence of the clergy of the established church.—7. The domestic irreligion of the great.

The history of modern Europe has demonstrated, that the ignorance and envy of the common people are sure sources of establishing erroneous opinions respecting religion; and, as it is not the peculiar boast of this country, that the understandings, even of the lowest members of society, are enlarged by all the aids of education and by its benign effects, or are exempt in a remarkable degree from the vice of envy, we are not to be surprized, that the existence of those evils may be brought forward as one of the causes which have afforded great facility to the Methodists for prosecuting the vast designs which they have formed against the established church. To indispose the minds of men towards any institution, religious or civil, the most effectual way, we take it for granted, is to exaggerate its abuses: and how often do we meet in the publications of the Methodists the insinuation, and in their preachings, the avowal, although it be an article of their creed to write or to speak nothing against our church establishment, that bishops, in the plenitude of their wealth, their power, their dignity, their arrogance, lose all recollection of the apostolic mandate, " to be blameless, not greedy of filthy lucre, nor lifted up with pride and self-conceit;" and that, instead of cherishing the poor, and considering them as their brethren, they have no other object than to amass wealth, and to aggrandize their own families? yet these accusations, the makers of which justly subject themselves to the weighty charge of wilfully violating the sacred obligations of truth, rarely fail to experience a most favourable reception with beings whose mental faculties, for the want of cultivation, exceed but little the cattle which they drive.

We know it to be generally conceived, that it is not common to envy those with whom we cannot easily be placed in comparison. The peasant, it may be justly imagined, would indulge in no animosity against the bishop, whose walk of life is so different to his: yet, from crafty men ingrafting their own pernicious prejudices upon his ignorant and unsuspicious mind, he is taught to view the episcopal bench with as much ill-will as if it had given him the most serious provocation to malice. This feeling of the common people, generally speaking, may be produced as a strong and conclusive proof of the necessity of giving them the advantages of education; for though envy be a weed more easily planted than plucked up, we are sanguine enough to believe, that had the means of improving the understandings of the poor been more encouraged, it could never have been nurtured in their bosoms; or at least the bulk of them, we trust, would then have derived this important knowledge from being instructed in the art of reading, that difference of rank in the church was by God's own appointment, and consequently essential to the well-being of society; and that though the high magistrates of the church could not be measured after the standard of those in the apostolical age, the difference lies more in a variation of modes and manners of life, than in any departure from the learning, charity, and benevolence, which characterized the saints of the primitive church.

In confirmation of this remark, we need only look to the valuable publications on matters of religion and morality which have proceeded from the pens of so many of the reverend bench; to their patronage and support of almost every charitable institution in the kingdom; and the laudable and public-spirited use which they make of the greater part of their revenues.

Reasoning from this last fact, the labourer and artizan would have seen through that detestable cant of hypocrisy, which would persuade them, that it so deeply - compassionated their state, as to hope the period would come, when the whole of episcopal property might be confiscated for their benefit; but which at the same time could drain them of their last shilling for the use of the Tabernacle. Can any rational being read, and not be filled with indignation and horror at the dangerous influence gained over the minds of ignorant people by these fanatics, that a poor man with a family, earning *only twenty-eight shillings a week, had made two donations, of ten guineas each, to the missionary fund**! This total indifference to the first of all tender and social ties, in the case of this infatuated individual, forcibly reminds us of the methodistical exclamations of old Lady Lambeth, in the Hypocrite: " How has he weaned me from all temporal connections ; my heart is now set upon nothing sublunary, and I thank Heaven I am so insensible to every thing in this vain world, that I could see my son, my daughters, my brothers, my grandchildren, all expire before me, and mind it no more than the going out of so many snuffs of a candle."

* See the Evangelical Magazine, for this extraordinary fact.

The clergyman of the established church but seldom dwells in his discourses upon the interference of Divine Providence in particular instances, unless they are closely interwoven with the downfall of empires, or any other revolution which may affect the happiness, or misery of millions: not that he affirms the universe to be ruled only by general laws, or denies the inspection and regard to terrestrial affairs of Him "who is about our path, and about our bed, and spieth out all our ways;" "without whom not a sparrow falls to the ground, and with whom the very hairs of our head are all numbered*." He knows God to be omnipresent, all-wise, and all-powerful, capable of governing and directing all things upon earth with equal ease, whether they be great or small; but that he thinks to insist upon the immediate interposition of his Almighty Power, upon every trifling occasion, would lead to the adoption of opinions repugnant to his moral justice, and therefore to true piety.

The Methodist preacher, however, shuts his ears against this sort of reasoning; what enlightened minds have considered as the innocent amusements of a leisure

* "Who sees with equal eye, as God of all,
　A hero perish, or a sparrow fall."

Essay on Man.

hour, his gloomy soul turns from with as much pious horror, as if they were polluted with the stain of idolatry: nay, God's avenging providence, if we listen to his narrations, would seem to follow those indulgences. In the Evangelical Magazine, which seems to be established for no other purpose than the admission of the most extravagant fictions of the *children of light and grace*, the *dear people*, the *elect*, the *people of God*, the Pharasaical names by which the votaries of Methodism distinguish themselves from the rest of mankind, we are instructed to believe, that a clergyman, for committing the heinous sin of playing a game of cards, was punished by instant death: " and it is worthy of remark," says the writer, " that, within a very few years, this was the third character in the neighbourhood which had been summoned from the card-table to the bar of God!"

We read also in the Methodists' Magazine, that to the justice of offended Heaven one of their preachers, before his conversion, ascribes the accident of dislocating his shoulder in partaking of the healthy exercise of dancing*. Let us take also the following instance,

---

* It is a moot point, if Wesley or Whitfield be the most violent in their condemnation of that amusement: the latter more than once says, in his Letters, that *dancers please the devil in every step;* and he elsewhere

from among many others equally satisfactory and important, of the encouragement which the Deity gave to the Father of Methodism, (need I add the name of Wesley,) to proceed in his evangelical undertaking: " My horse was exceedingly lame ; we could not discern what it was that was amiss, and yet he could scarce set his foot on the ground.   My head ached more than it had done for some months, (what I here aver is the naked fact, let every man account for it as he sees good ;) I then thought, cannot God heal either man or beast by any means, or *without any !*—immediately my weariness and head-ache ceased, and my horse's lameness in the same instant; nor did he halt any more, either that day or the next*."   *Ab uno disce omnes.*

But whoever expects to read of the interests of Methodism being materially advanced without any miraculous interposition, will be woefully disappointed. All sorts of disorders, acute as well as chronical, disappeared on the approach of their founder : and a close and impartial investigation of his journal warrants us in concluding, that he principally founded his pre-

---

congratulates himself upon having demolished Satan's strongest holds in Philadelphia, the Dancing School Assemblies, and Music Meetings, those houses of *Baal.*

* See Journal from July 20, 1735, to October 28, 1754, p. 10.

tensions to the character of a saint and apostle upon the numerous, pointed, and particular proofs of the divine approbation, which he affirms were shewn to him in the course of his ministry. Conformably then to the belief, that the seal of Heaven was set to the truth of Mr. Wesley's mission, his infatuated and ambitious biographer*, Dr. Coke, in opposition to every dictate of common sense, and to every restraint of common shame, scruples not to tell us, that when his preaching was interrupted by the clamour and violence of a London mob, it was the declaration of Sir John Ganson, and the other Middlesex magistrates, that they had orders *from above* to do him justice whenever he applied to them.

There are some men who would depreciate the highest excellencies of Christianity, if they could be depreciated by the manner in which they attempt to

---

* Without the influence, the name and even office of a bishop seems to have been inadequate to the aspiring views of this fierce sectary.—*See Nightingale's Portraiture of Methodism*, p. 402, 406. Whoever finds himself hovering on the brink of Methodism, we would seriously exhort to peruse this work, from which several of the facts stated in this Essay are taken. The impulse of an ardent mind seems to have urged the author of it to become one of the evangelical preachers, before his reasoning faculties had attained their full maturity: in that character, however, he has been enabled to divulge most of the " secrets of the prison-house," and justice requires, and truth permits us to add, *that none but the bigot and enthusiast* can complain of his partiality.—*See his Life of Wesley*, p. 246.

set them forth; and among this number may be surely reckoned that man, who could seek to twist such an influence from an expression, which could have no other meaning, but that the king would not permit any of his subjects to be persecuted on account of their religion. In many instances it is extremely difficult to distinguish between the delusions of enthusiasm, and the artifices of imposture; but here the traces of the latter are so plainly marked, as to preclude the possibility of mistake.

From the foregoing facts it must be now sufficiently evident, that this doctrine of the immediate and supernatural interference of Providence, has effectually contributed to the increase of Methodism: it cannot then excite our astonishment, that the Methodist preacher should disdain having recourse to the mild arts of persuasion and reasoning, or what he terms *head knowledge*, for the purpose of calling sinners to repentance, when this doctrine presents him with the means of adopting such a quick and efficacious mode for their conversion. How flat and unprofitable are all appeals to the sense and reason of mankind, in competition with a doctrine which, like this, so forcibly addresses itself to the strongest of the passions, which announces instant death to the players of whist, and dislocated shoulders to the lovers of dancing! Is not this alone sufficient to shake the stability of our established pulpits, from whence we are never assailed with the fears of such punishments for such gigantic crimes?—but, in their place, we hear such gross and pernicious *mistakes* as the following:—That there is a Providence* which controuls all human events, and oftentimes brings good out of evil; but that it would clash with some of the moral attributes of the Deity, to believe in a miraculous interference of providence on every trifling occasion:—to another world we must look then for the correction of all the apparent irregularities of the present system†, where the good will receive their due reward, and the wicked their due punishment. " Let not thine heart envy sinners, but be thou in the fear of the Lord all the day long; for surely there is an end, and thine expectation shall not be cut off."—*Prov. xxiii.* 17, 18. Such are the irra-

* It was a saying of the Emperor Marcus, which may be mentioned with the highest approbation, that he would not endure to live one day in the world, if he did not believe it to be under the government of Providence.

† " Cum res hominum tantâ caligine volvi adspicerem, *lætosque diu florere nocentes vexarique pios, labefacta cadebat religio,*" is the language of all those who infer with the atheist, that from the unequal distribution of moral good and evil, the universe must be without an intelligent Ruler.

tional and impious notions of these *dumb* dogs*, the *christian epithet* applied by the evangelical teachers to the clergy of the church of England: no wonder then that our pastors should incur the severe censure and reprobation of men, so renowned for superiority of learning and liberality of sentiments, as the Methodists are admitted to be both by friends and foes!

The second doctrine by which the Methodists have so widely diffused their faith, is the doctrine of inward impulse or emotions, or, as they term it, *experience;* which certainly does not require any minute discussion or profound remarks to shew, that if preached among the low and simple, it must engender in them the most excessive superstition, or interested cunning: for, if credulous and ignorant men are taught to ascribe every internal feeling to the immediate agency of the Supreme Being, there can be little doubt but that those who embrace this doctrine will be apt to fall into the vice of rashness and enthusiasm; to mistake phrenzy for illu-

---

* No person, among the Methodists, shall call another heretic, bigot, or any other disrespectful name, on any account, for difference of sentiment. *See the fourth clause in the twenty-ninth section of the General Minister, cited by Nightingale, p. 263.* From the *scrupulous* manner in which the preachers of the Tabernacle adhere to this rule, the difference between their souls and those of the established clergy of England may be easily estimated.

mination, and the delusion of a distempered brain for
the impulse of the spirit. The line of demarcation
here, indeed, is so small between the regions of enthusiasm and madness, as to be almost imperceptible.

During the meeting of a love-feast*, it is usual for
men and women to communicate their *sweet experiences.*
" I remember," says the author of the Portraiture of
Methodism, "when I first attended one of these meetings, I thought surely a new species of beings had
come among us in the form of men, to tell what was
passing in the realms of light and in the regions of
darkness." The preacher first opens the imposing
scene by relating his own experience to the congregation: when he has astonished his mute and im-
movable auditors, with a full account of his apostacy
from the christian faith to the *first drawings of the
Spirit,* another " dreamer of dreams" rises, to tell
what the Lord has done for his soul. Sometimes the
effects of a decent education, or a sense of modesty,
will occasion a young female, in reciting her trials,
temptations, backslidings, conversion, present feelings,
and future resolutions, to this assembly of enthusiasts,

---

* We are told, that Mr. Wesley borrowed the practice of holding the
Agapæ, or *feasts* of love, from the Moravian brethren. —*See Nightingale, p.* 201.

to betray that sort of perplexity which may be interpreted into reluctance to approve this public confession, and yet into a terror not to make it.

Αἴδεσθεν μὲν ἀνήνασθαι, δεῖσαν δ' ὑποδέχθαι.
Iliad, Lib. vii. v. 93.

In such a situation, the feelings of the hesitating female must be of the most agonizing kind; for it is the unanimous sentiment of those who have arrived at christian perfection and entire sanctification, that this unwillingness is solely to be attributed to the influence of the devil: it is but rare, however, that instances of this kind occur. In general the votaries of the Tabernacle discover such eagerness to announce the miraculous circumstances which led to their separation from the *carnal people, the people of this world*, that, from their frequent practice of rising at the same time, the preacher is often called upon to determine who shall have the precedence.

Of the nature of the confessions that take place at the meeting of *the select bands*, we are not permitted to speak, since they are as closely guarded as the secrets of free-masonry; we may, however, suppose them to be of the most edifying kind, as we are told that these bands consist only of members who have attained to what is called a state of perfection, or, in other words, those who never, *on any account, or any occasion, or temptation whatsoever, commit the slightest sin in thought, word, or deed**. It is recorded of Augustus Cæsar, that after a long and diligent enquiry into every part of his immense empire, he found but one man who was reputed never to have uttered a falsehood; upon which account he was deemed worthy to be appointed chief sacrificer in the Temple of Truth†. Now we would as readily believe, that the Emperor found whole provinces peopled with beings who never spoke an untruth upon any occasion whatsoever, as the real existence of the foregoing perfections among the select bands. What! shall we infants in goodness‡, but

---

* " Through lustrations and purgative fires it seems our Methodists arrive at perfection, visions of God and Angels, ingulfments into the Deity, union with God, yea, and being God. That Mr. Wesley must mean such a perfection as implieth *absolute freedom from sin and inward corruption, such as was in Christ,* appears by his earnest dispute with the Moravians, and contending that in this respect, the servant may be as his master; hence, saith the woman in a high fever, I am very ill, but I am very well, for I am united to Jesus: my beloved hath cleansed me from all sin, I am washed, I am cleansed; the enemy may come, but he hath no part in me."—*See the Enthusiasm of Methodists and Papists compared, vol. XI. p. 207.*

† Vide Causabon, H. C. tom. I. Lib. xi. p. 45.

‡ The Methodists are in the constant habit of making triumphant appeals to the Bible, as they conceive, for the justification of their faith and practice. Let them try the experiment in the following instance,

giants in sin, impiously dare to affirm that, in this
dissolute age, are to be found among us those in whom
every religious and social perfection is blended; when
the wisest and best are full of spots and blemishes,
and when such is the incurable frailty of human nature,
that even he* upon whom the Holy Ghost, as the
spirit and guide of truth, had descended, could not
even then conduct himself so as to be free of the
slightest sin in thought, word, or deed. Moderation
towards those who differ from us in religious opinions,
is a feeling highly amiable, and cannot be too assi-
duously cultivated: yet, if ever there was an occasion
to justify a departure from it, it is surely against a sect
whose religion is fanaticism, and whose arrogant claims
to the real practice of superior piety and virtue may

and they will find many such sentences to this effect : " For there is no
man that sinneth not."—1 *Kings*. " If thou, Lord, should mark ini-
quities, who should stand?"—*Psalm cxxx.* 3. We had hitherto understood, that the necessity of a Redeemer was solely founded upon this
universal depravity of mankind, and consequent liability to punishment.

* We allude to the fallibility, or rather to the gross prevarication of
St. Peter, who, for fear of offending the Jews, withdrew himself from
the Gentiles, as if it had been unlawful for him to hold conversation
with uncircumcised persons; notwithstanding he knew, and was fully
satisfied, that his divine Master had broken down the wall of partition
between the Jew and the Gentile. " But when Peter was come to
Antioch, I withstood him to the face, because he was to be blamed."—
See St. Paul's Epistle to the Galatians, chap. ii. 11.

be, with as much justice disputed, as that scheme of Doctor Darwin's to uncommon sagacity, which proposed to mend the climates of the frigid and torrid zones, by towing ice islands from the pole to the equator, and of regulating the winds by means of chemical mixtures. The following passage in that first of French comedies, *Le Tartuffe*, so finely points out the distinction between hypocrisy and devotion, and is here so particularly applicable, that the reader of discernment will overlook its length for the noble zeal with which it pleads the cause of true religion :—

> " Il est de faux devots, ainsi que de faux braves,
> Et comme on ne voit pas qu' a l'honneur les conduit,
> Les vrays braves, soient ceux qui font beaucoup bruit,
> Les bons et vrays devots, qu'on doit suivre à la trace,
> Ne sont pas ceux aussi qui font tant de grimace.
> Hé quoi ! Vous ne ferez nulle distinction
> Entre l'hypocrisie, et la devotion ?
> Vous les voulez traiter d'un semblable language,
> Et rendre même honneur au masque qu' au visage,
> Egaler l'artifice à la sincerité,
> Confondre l'apparence avec la vérité,
> Et la le fantôme autant que la personne,
> Et la fausse monnoye, à l'égal de la bonne ?
> Les hommes, la plupart, sont étrangement faits,
> Dans la juste nature on ne les voit jamais.
> La raison a pour eux, des bornes, trop petites,
> En chaque charactere ils passent ses limites,
> Et la plus noble chose, ils la gatent souvent,
> Pour la vouloir outrer et pousser trop avant."

The third doctrine which calls for notice among the Methodists, is that of justification *by faith alone;* a doctrine which Mr. Wesley had imbibed from his Moravian brethren, and insisted upon with great vehemence during the whole of his subsequent life; and which his followers unremittingly labour to prove our clergy have wilfully neglected and deserted, because they do not constantly press it upon our attention in their discourses*;—because they think it to be

* In reviewing the article of our church upon the doctrine of justification by faith only, so similar in its object and tendency to the tenet of the Lutherans, we must never separate it from the doctrine of *penitence;* for in the apology of their confession, those reformists made the most explicit and formal declaration of a rejection of all faith, except such as exists in the contrite heart: when, therefore, they maintained a justification by faith alone, it was far from their intention to reject repentance, and every good disposition associated with it, but merely to mark the abhorrence excited in them by the doctrine of the Papists, that the remission of sin was to be acquired by the merit of the individual. In an exact conformity then of opinion with the Lutherans upon this point, our church pronounces, that we are accounted righteous before God, for the merit of our Lord and Saviour Jesus Christ, by faith, and not for our own works and deserving: yet it is worthy of constant recollection, that the very definition which she gives of the word *faith*, in a homily composed at the period this article was framed, is powerfully adapted to counteract any of the mischievous effects arising from the interpretation of this article by the Methodists; since, in the homily to which I refer, *faith* is defined to be, a trust in God, that our sins are expiated by the atonement of Christ; not when we believe them to be thus expiated, but whensoever we, repenting truly, return to him with our whole heart, steadfastly determining with ourselves, through his grace, to obey and

their great duty to teach their flocks, that *faith* in Christ *is the foundation* of our title to Heaven, but that *good works* are absolutely necessary to a place in his everlasting kingdom. We will say then a few words respecting the historical part of this doctrine, before we attempt to shew its mischievous tendency in the hands of such people as the Methodists.

In our first general separation from the church of Rome, the immoderate zeal of some well-meaning but mistaken divines, had pushed the doctrine of justification by faith alone, even to a height of extravagance, under the notion of providing an antidote for the poison which they conceived was instilled by the papal doctrine of merits; and it is well known, that the puritans in the civil wars carried this doctrine into a most dangerous and impure *Antinomianism*, since it suited their crafty purposes, first to depreciate morality,

serve him, in keeping his commandments ; and such it wisely and emphatically adds, *is the true faith which the scripture doth so much commend:* as if too, the framers of this article had foreseen how much the true and sole meaning of it would be eluded and perverted by a swarm of fanatics, they annexed, in the fullness of their wisdom, the succeeding article, in 1562 ; which in a short, simple, and decisive manner, teaches *that good works are indispensable for the attainment of salvation.* The mutual connection therefore of these two articles, and dependance upon each other, will never, I trust, be forgotten by all those who wish to be regarded as sober christians, and firm friends to the establishment.

and then to dispense with it: when, however, monarchy was restored, the church of England, to prevent as far as was in its power, the gospel principle of faith from being again abused, wisely endeavoured to restore morality to its injured rights; accordingly the most eminent divines of that day never failed to preach up morality, as forming no less an essential part of the christian system than the gospel principle of faith. The effects of their discourses were soon apparent in the conduct of the people: taught by these truly learned and pious men the duties which they owed to God, to themselves, and to society, the flame of fanaticism no longer burnt in their breasts, and they became once more satisfied, and obedient, laborious, sober christians. Such was the unequivocal good imparted to the nation at large by these divines, who, because they taught their auditors to seek their way to Heaven by acts of charity, as well as by high professions of faith, received from the zealots of the times the inappropriate name of *latitudinarians*.

But since Methodism has reared her ugly head, the doctrine of practical righteousness is utterly out of fashion among the greater part of the lower orders of the community. Now what an irreparable calamity this circumstance alone, of insisting upon the necessity of faith, and not of good works, may produce to this country at a future period, if this sect should grow with its growth, and strengthen with its strength, is for wiser heads to predict ; since the most common sense must know, that fanaticism is soon exchanged for atheism among those who are taught that they may be saved without, nay, in defiance of, the moral law. Perhaps we may here be told, that in preaching faith, the Methodists preach at the same time good works, since the one cannot possibly exist without the other : not so, however, is the conclusion of their infallible oracle, Mr. Wesley, and therefore we may presume to add, not theirs also; but that we may avoid the imputation, as well as the danger, of misrepresenting his opinion upon this important subject, we shall give it in his own words:—*True religion does not consist in any, or all these three things,—the living harmless, using the means of grace, and doing much good. A man may do all this, and yet have no true religion*[*]: yet, until our eyes had met with this declaration of the modern St. Paul[+], we had foolishly enough conceived, that pure

[*] See Journal, from November 14th, 1739, to September 30th, 1741, p. 11, 12.

[+] An appellation by no means displeasing to those in the Wesleyan connection.

or true religion, and undefiled before God and the Father, is this: " to visit the fatherless and widow in their afflictions, and to keep himself unspotted from the world*."   And such hitherto has been our heathen ignorance, (for our readers, no more than ourselves, must flatter themselves that they have any real pretensions to the name of christians, unless *they have been called to a knowledge of Christ, under a sermon of Mr. Wesley, or his followers+,)* that whenever our spiritual pastors, appointed by law, have exhorted us to remember, that faith without works would not secure the possession of eternal happiness, we had imagined they equally inculcated the precepts of morality and of the Gospel‡. " What doth it profit, my brethren, though a man say he hath faith, and have not works; can faith save him ? If a brother or sister be naked, and destitute of daily food, and one of you say unto them, depart in peace, be you warmed and filled; notwithstanding ye give them not those things which

* St. James' Epistle, chap. i. v. 27.

+ *See Evangelical Magazine, p* 176, for an account of Mr. Robinson's being first admitted into the church of Christ, under a sermon by Mr. Venn.—*See likewise this Magazine, p.* 380, for the introduction of Christianity into the parish of Launton, near Bicester, in the year 1807.

‡ St. James' Epistle, chap. xi. v. 14, 17.

are needful to the body, what doth it profit? Even so faith, if it hath not works, is dead, being alone."

Upon so important a branch of the Methodistical hierarchy as that of class-meetings is, the reader will look perhaps for that sort of detail which will serve more to satisfy than to excite his curiosity; that he may not then be entirely disappointed in that expectation, we shall lay before him some account of the origin of them, before we proceed to enter into a survey of their present nature and objects.

The origin of class-meetings was instituted at first with a view to effect only a temporary purpose; but the substantial benefits which they imparted soon made them common throughout the whole connection. " I was talking," says the father of Methodism, " with several of the society in Bristol, concerning the means of paying the debts there, (which had been incurred by building, &c.) when one stood up and said, Let every member of the society give a penny a week, till all are paid. Another answered, But many of them are poor, and cannot afford to do it. Then said he, put eleven of the poorest with me, and if they can give any thing, well; I will call on them weekly, and if they can give nothing, then I will give for them as well as for myself; and each of you call on eleven of your neighbours weekly, receive what they give, and make up what is wanting! It was done. In a while some of these informed me they found such and such an one did not live as he ought! It struck me immediately, this is the thing, the very thing we have wanted so long." For the reader is here to learn, that before this plan had been suggested, Mr. Wesley's sharp-sighted eyes had spied out that some wolves had crept into his flock, or, in other words, there were a few, *mirabile dictu*, who happened not to be quite animated with a zeal like his for the support and propagation of the true faith: this plan, therefore, presented a most favourable opportunity which Mr. Wesley had long ardently sought, but hitherto sought in vain, of getting rid of men, whose lukewarmness he was at times apprehensive might even communicate itself to those who most faithfully executed his mandates, and imitated his example; for lukewarmness was ever contemplated by him with more horror than opposition. " He that is not with me, is against me," said the scourge of Europe to the Elector of Saxony, when he wished to be ranked by him as a neutral power: and upon that point Buonaparte and the warrior of God seem to have been of the same opinion. But to finish our extract—

" Accordingly," proceeds the saint, " I called together all the leaders of the classes, (as we used to term them and their companies,) and desired that each would make a particular enquiry into the behaviour of those whom he saw weekly; they did so. Many disorderly walkers were detected: some turned from the evil of their ways, some were put away from us; many saw it with fear, and rejoiced unto God with reverence. As soon as possible the same method was used in London, and all other places: evil men were detected and reproved: they were borne with for a season. If they forsook their sins, we received them gladly; if they obstinately persisted therein, it was openly declared that they were not of us. The rest mourned and prayed for them—and yet rejoiced, that as far as in us lay the scandal was rolled away from the society." Such was the rise of class-meetings; and as Mr. Wesley's disciples were fully persuaded that he was born for no other purpose but the spiritual happiness of the whole world, *whenever therefore he spake, it was done; whatever he commanded, stood fast.*

The fair sex now compose a part of the class-meeting of the present day; like the female quaker overseers, they take charge of their own sex only; but as men and women are generally associated together upon this occasion, the leader is of course a brother. Prayer and singing being concluded, he proceeds to arrest their attention by a circumstantial account of his conflicts with the world, the flesh and the devil, during the preceding week; and his experience is generally terminated with the assurance, that the ruling passion of his soul is the desire of walking closely with Christ*. " After all, my dear brethren, I still find a determination in my soul to press forward for the mark of the prize of my high calling of God in Christ Jesus: he is still precious; his word is as ointment poured forth. After all my short comings, my doubts and anxieties, my wanderings, weakness, and weariness, his Spirit still whispers to my heart—thou art black, but comely: open thy mouth wide, and I will fill it. Make haste, my beloved, and be thou like a rose, or to a young hart upon the mountains of spice! So I still may say to my sweet Jesus,

> " I hold thee with a trembling hand,
> " And will not let thee go."

* Such however is the presumptive holiness of Mr. Whitfield, that he is not satisfied without having a still nearer intercourse with God : *he seems disposed to penetrate even into the arcana of the Godhead. " In the morning,"* says Mr. Whitfield, *" I talked with God as a man talketh with his friend ! ! ! !"—See this most extraordinary passage in the Enthusiasm of Papists and Methodists, &c. vol. I. p. 39.*

After this peroration, the next step in the pious business of the evening is for the leader to make a categorical enquiry into the state of every soul present; a mode of proceeding which, in our humble apprehension, is attended with far more injurious consequences than was ever occasioned among us by that relict of papal superstition, auricular confession. But the Methodists are so spotless, so exercised in the habits of chastity, and in all their institutions the traces of perfect wisdom are so discoverable, that nothing but the ignorance of malice, or of infidelity, could affect to believe those confessions were so far from inspiring the love of truth, modesty, and all the other moral virtues that they very often produced, especially among the women,—effects which the real friends of christianity would blush to mention. The aid of vocal music is then summoned; and in such hymns as the following the languishing spirit of devotion is raised up to a pitch of enthusiasm, which none but the enemies of our religion could possibly insult and ridicule.

A MOURNER BROUGHT TO THE BIRTH.

> " I'll weary thee with my complaint,
> " Here at thy feet for ever lie ;
> " With longing sick, with groaning faint,
> " O give me love, or else I die."

REJOICING.

" My God, I am thine! What a comfort divine!
" What a blessing to know that my Jesus is mine!
" In the heavenly Lamb, thrice happy I am ;
" And my heart it doth dance at the sound of his name.

" True pleasures abound in the rapturous sound,
" And whoever hath found it, hath paradise found ;
" My Jesus to know, and feel his blood flow,
" 'Tis life everlasting, 'tis heaven below.

" Yet onward I haste to the heavenly feast ;
" That, that is the fulness ! but this is the taste ;
" And this I shall prove, till with joy I remove
" To the heaven of heavens, in Jesus's love* !"

———

" Ah ! why did I so late thee know,
" Thee, lovelier than the sons of men?
" Ah ! why did I no sooner go
" To thee, the only ease in pain?
" Ashamed I sigh, and only mourn,
" That I so late to thee did turn."

* During a dangerous illness of Mr. Wesley, he is thus addressed by
Mr. Whitfield : " but if the decree is gone forth, that you must now
fall asleep in Jesus, may he kiss your soul away, and give you to die in
the embraces of triumphant love,"—See Dr. Coke's Life of Wesley,
page 310.

"   O love ! I languish at·thy stay !
     " I pine for thee with lingering smart ;
     " Weary and faint, through long delay,
     " When wilt thou come into my heart ?
     " From sin and sorrow set me free,
     " And swallow up my soul in thee !"

Under the impression of these pious songs, devotion kindles into one strong and prevailing passion of enthusiasm*: the unconverted, or those who labour in the pangs of the new birth, and those who are groaning for full redemption, then feel in themselves that particular disposition of mind which prompts them to give a free vent to the soft meltings of the heart†. In

---

* It is the opinion of many competent judges, that a little more attention on the part of our parochial clergy to church music, might be productive of very good effects among the people. " While I was describing to the primate Robinson some of these motley congregations, and the unwearied efforts of Mr. Benson for reclaiming them, he said to me in his plain and pointed way, ' if you wish to get these people back again, you must *sing them in*, they will not come to your preaching ; arguments will do nothing with them ; but they have itching ears, and will listen to a hymn or an anthem ; and as you have an organ, such as it is, you must set to work and assemble the best singers which your place affords."—*See Supplement to the Memoirs of Richard Cumberland, page* 22.

† " Mr. Wesley's inspired disciples (justly observes the author of *the Enthusiasm of Methodists and Papists compared, vol. II. p.* 141) seem like those brazen vessels in Dodona, so placed, that if one was struck or moved, the sound and motion was immediately communicated to all the rest."

short, every circumstance here is admirably fitted to prevent members from sinking into listlessness, and not less adapted for the purposes of conversion: yet the rational advocate for the establishment, who views this meeting with an unprejudiced eye, sees nothing in it but a pretended zeal for religion, mixed with the wildest extravagances of error, and cannot therefore be surprized at the number of ignorant persons flocking to the standard of Methodism, so long as a class-meeting exists to encourage the wanderings of fancy, and the visions of fanaticism*.

In enumerating the causes which have assisted the influence of Methodism, it might be justly regarded as an unpardonable omission, were we only slightly to mention the extemporaneous preaching of its ministers; since, we will venture to say, that here they have attacked the church on the side in which it is most vulnerable. It will not be denied, that the bulk of mankind are affected mostly by externals. It is not the matter of a discourse, but the manner of its de-

---

* "Cherish *true Religion*," piously exclaims the first of British Statesmen, and one of the firmest believers and defenders of christianity, " as preciously as you will fly with abhorrence and contempt superstition and enthusiasm. The first is the perfection and glory of human nature, the two last the depravation and disgrace of it."—*See Lord Chatham's admirable Letters to his Nephew, p.* 24.

livery, which is calculated to make an impression upon their senses. The very ungraceful way, then, in which the generality of the clergy of the establishment deliver their sermons, may safely be pronounced to be one of the reasons for the people deserting the church for the conventicle.

But energy in the pulpit is stigmatized by the degrading epithets of foolish and theatrical. It is not orthodox to be animated in speaking of the nature and attributes of God; or of his blessed Son, the friend and saviour of mankind, who came down from Heaven to rescue us from sin and death. What! shall the senator, in the mere support of a turnpike bill, and the lawyer, in discussing a dry legal point, express warm feelings as much by their face and gesticulation as by their voice?—and shall the servants of the Most High, in descanting upon such sublime topics as those we have just now mentioned, be still distinguished for their inanimate elocution? The great secret, says Quintilian*, of moving the passions, is to be moved ourselves; but how is it to be expected that piety should grow warm, when most of our clergy pray and preach as if they were repeating words, instead of in-

* Summa enim circa movendos affectus in hoc posita est, ut moveamur ipsi.—*Lib. vi. cap. ii.*

culcating sentiments?—when they suffer one dull mo-
notony to pervade every period of their discourse,
for fear of being styled theatrical and affected? Let
those who consider it almost a species of heresy to
arouse the attention, and engage the heart by the genuine look and voice of passion, only cast their eyes
upon the number of schismatics who have departed
from the orthodox faith, and then determine whether
tame or animated pastors have most contributed to the
honour and increase of the church. Such powerful
effects may be traced, even from the appearance of
being in earnest in the pulpit, that we are fully persuaded, if the generality of the Methodists did not
mistake rant for energy, instead of drawing after them
the low and middling orders of society, we should see
their folly and imposition countenanced even by persons
of rank and fashion. Whitfield surely would not
have numbered among his auditors a Chesterfield and
a Bolingbroke, if he had owed his celebrity as a preacher
entirely to stage trick and extravagant grimace.

If then that pillar of Calvinian Methodism should
have succeeded in making more converts by the graces
of his delivery than by his doctrines, how just a matter
is it of regret to all who regard the establishment with
the most friendly eye, that so many of its clergy, from

the sole dread of being denominated popular preachers, should still afford some just ground for wits and libertines to call their churches public dormitories, when the greater part of them possess knowledge and abilities sufficient to render the most essential service to truth, virtue, and religion: for it is not, we contend, the rhapsodical nonsense* which the Methodist preachers pour forth for one or two hours without the assistance of book or paper, and the consequent notion among the ignorant, that God's spirit resides in them and speaks from their mouth; no; nor it is not the fulminations which these ecclesiastical mountebanks let fly, without mercy or prudence, of eternal tortures to the lukewarm and wavering, nor that disgusting bitterness of spirit which leads them to deal damnation around the land, that half so much has brought over the multitude to their party, as the fervour and animation with which their perfect cant is delivered†.

* To such as are unwilling hearers of it, we would wish to call to their remembrance the following consolatory couplet of Mr. Herbert, of pious memory :—

——————— If all wants sense,
God takes a text, and preacheth patience.

† In a printed sermon of Mr. Adam Clark's, a man of great authority, we believe, among the Methodists, and certainly deemed by them of great talents, the following expressions, we suppose, are designed at

As the Methodists are, in as full a degree, possessed with the spirit of proselytism as the Roman Catholics ever were, and this mischievous zeal in them, we may remark by the way, wants even the wretched plea of the former, namely, the belief of the infallibility of their church,—they soon found, that to rivet firmly the bonds of subjection on the multitude which their preaching had first imposed, it was also necessary that their lives should assume the appearance of the most rigid sanctity. Agreeably to this notion the following

once to terrify and subdue into an implicit obedience those whose vices, or, we should rather say, frailties, have been considered by the preacher to affect the character of the society :—" A damned spirit. A devil damned in the abyss of perdition, in the burning pool which spouts cataracts of fire !—Sinners may lose their time in disputing against the *reality* of hell-fire, till awakened to a sense of their folly, by finding themselves plunged into what God calls the lake that burns with fire and brimstone.—Many are desirous of seeing an inhabitant of the other world, or they wish to *converse* with one, to know what passes there : curiosity and infidelity are as insatiable as they are unreasonable. Here, however, God steps out of the common way to indulge them. You wish to see a disembodied spirit ! Make way ! Here is a damned soul, which Christ has waked from the hell of fire ! Hear him ! Hear him tell of his torments ! Hear him utter his anguish ! Listen to the sighs and groans which are wrung from his soul by the torture he endures ! Hear him asking for a drop of water to cool his burning tongue ! telling you that he is tormented in that flame, and warning you to repent, that you may come not into that place of torture ! How solemn is this warning ! How awful this voice ! Hear the groans of this damned soul, and be alarmed !"

questions, among many others, are proposed to the candidate for their ministry:—" Do you enjoy a clear manifestation of the love of God to your soul? Have you constant power over all sin? Are you determined to employ all your time in the work of God?"

In this last question, the secret dread which the Methodists entertain of all human learning is sufficiently evident to the most careless observer. The acquisition of knowledge is, indeed, always fatal to the reign of fanaticism and superstition: Mr. Wesley was therefore perfectly right in not making his lay preachers scholars*, as he was well aware, that the improvement of their understandings by reading and reflection would, sooner or later, lead them to discover that there were as many false zealots in religion, as false patriots in politics. But perhaps it would be more respectful to those friends of the dear Redeemer+ to conclude, that

* The Methodists seem to have as much aversion to scholarship, as the schoolmen had to quote scripture in their public disputations. M. Menage, that indefatigable collector of literary anecdotes, informs us, that he found the following notice in the register of the faculty at Paris: " Solida die sexta Julii ab aurora ad vespera fuit disputatum, et *quidem tam subtiliter, ut ne verbum de tota scriptura fuerit allegatum.*"

+ For the free us of this familiar and irreverent expression, in the Evangelical Magazine, p. 268, see an account of the religious hoy, which sets off every week for Margate.

they would be far from holding in utter contempt all knowledge which was not useful to salvation, unless they had received an especial communication *from above*, that poetry offered nothing but false or common thoughts, expressed in an artificial style; history, doubts and uncertainties; physics, darkness; morality, obvious truths or dangerous paradoxes; and metaphysics, vain and frivolous subtleties.

If then these inspired teachers of the Gospel are instructed to despise the erudition of this world, its pleasures we may of course expect to find entitled to a large share of their detestation; balls, plays, and every species of public spectacles, are considered as so many temptations to divert us from the path of holiness, in the judgment of these severe reformers— " Dancing is not fit for a being who is preparing himself for eternity;" and the play-house is characterized as the habitation of the devil.

Mr. Wilberforce, the great advocate for the Methodists, is pleased to say, that " even when moral principles are inculcated on the stage, they are not such as a christian ought to cherish in his bosom, but such as must be his daily endeavour to extirpate; not those which Scripture warrants, but those which it condemns as false and spurious, being founded in pride and ambition, and the over-valuation of human favor*." In a former Essay an opportunity presented itself, of which we cheerfully availed ourselves, to offer our tribute of respect to the public character of this gentleman; while, as a writer upon the important subject of religion, we have no hesitation to say, that even his faults are derived from an excess of virtue. This declaration will then, or ought, to satisfy the most suspicious, that our objections to this most objectionable sentence must not be hastily and indiscriminately ascribed to any undue partiality for theatrical† amusements, but to a persuasion, that the spiritual zeal of the author has hurried him, in this instance, even beyond the bounds of truth and benevolence; for surely he will not assert, that all the precepts and axioms delivered by the genius of a Shakspeare, in those productions which will instruct and delight, and, we had almost dared to add, edify the most distant ages, are calculated to bring piety into disgrace.

* See a practical view of the prevailing religious system of professed Christians, p. 306.

† It would be difficult, even for Mr. Wilberforce to shew, that all the sentiments expressed by Portia, in the Merchant of Venice, and the Duke and Isabella, in Measure for Measure, are such as a Christian ought not to cherish in his bosom.

Many pieces are still tolerated, we grant, in which
we are at a loss to recognize the propriety of denomi-
nating the stage the school of morals and delicacy,
and which would justify the stern expression of St.
Augustin*, that " theatrical performances are the
blemishes of nature, the plague of reason, and the
ruin of virtue." We are sensible also, that a moral
sentence, tacked to the end of a play abounding in
licentious images, is calculated to do no more good than
a pious expression which drops from the mouth of a
dying man, whose whole life has been one uninterrupted scene of wickedness.

But though this be admitted, and a great deal more,
the shutting up our theatres would not a jot advance
the spiritual interests, either of the lower or the higher
classes of society; since the former would spend those
hours at the ale-house which could not be passed at
the theatre, and the latter be immersed more than
ever in a round of folly and dissipation. The moral
character of no people is solely formed by precepts;
we may discourse very wisely about the beauty of
virtue, and the deformity of vice, yet fail of exciting
even the attention of our audience, much less " to

* See De Civitate Dei, Lib. i. cap. xxxi.

ope the sacred source of sympathetic tears:" but the actual representation before us, of incidents in which vice is triumphant, or virtue injured or depressed, will always powerfully affect the best feelings of our nature. Whatever therefore contributes to inspire us with virtuous sentiments, and this the stage does, we contend, with all its defects, though its practical influence may not be very lasting, is surely not to be regarded as a " proof of our defective love of God;" at least, we believe, such is not the conclusion of the bulk of nominal christians, or, in other words, of those who are not illuminated by a single ray of the light of Methodism.

The pious indignation of Methodist preachers is not more excited by theatrical entertainments, than by gay apparel and sumptuous living*; but in censuring such things the profane may be tempted to suspect, that whatever fortune has placed beyond their reach is certain of incurring their hatred. It is indeed no sign of a very elevated mind, to substitute railing for reasoning, as they do, in speaking of all articles of luxury; but this conduct, it must be acknowledged, is very consistent in men who despise, or affect to

---

* See Mr. Wesley's general character of a Methodist.

despise, every enjoyment which is not of a spiritual nature. The reader will not then be astonished to hear, that those who are ambitious of superior sanctity, and who vainly aspire to " be all fair," to have no spot in them, consider, that the most certain way to conciliate the good-will of God in an eminent degree, is to renounce the delightful freedom of social intercourse, and to regard all trifling levity of discourse as a criminal abuse of the gift of speech. Active virtues with them are destitute of any value or efficacy, when put in competition with the merit of incessant prayer, which we have heard wise men call incessant indolence*; since the love of action is a principle interwoven, as it were, in our constitution, and the chief use of prayer is to implore the divine favour to our actions. We may push the observation still further upon the bad effects of incessant prayer, by concluding, that it

* Incessant praying might also be called excessive ignorance; for surely none but the most deluded enthusiast can expect to attain to an intimate acquaintance with God by prayer without study. " Let no one," says that profound philosopher and devout christian, Lord Bacon, " weakly imagine, that men can search too far, or be too well studied in the book of God's *words* and *works*, divinity and philosophy; but rather let them endeavour an endless progression in both, only applying all to charity, and not to pride; to use, not ostentation; without confounding the two different streams of philosophy and revelation together." *See Vol. I. p.* 18, *Shawe's edition.*

gradually and insensibly leads him who practises it into a presumptuous belief, that God has selected him as an instrument to instruct and reform mankind, till at last fanaticism has firmly established her dominion over his mind. It is related by Dionysius Halicarnassensis, that the first Romans, in order to prevent theological enthusiasm, enacted, that no one should be admitted into the sacerdotal office before he had accomplished his fiftieth year. If none became Methodist preachers before they had arrived at that age, we will venture to pronounce, that the true object of devotion, and the true spirit of it, would not now be utterly lost, as it is among them, in the futile and absurd opinion, that they alone are the distinguished favourites of the Father of the universe.

It will be no digression to conclude this part of our subject with describing one of the many ways by which the number of Methodists is augmented. To diffuse the faith of Mr. Wesley by every means in his power, is part of the sacred duty of a prayer leader or exhorter: accordingly, whenever he and his party come to a place where Methodism is embraced by none, or a few only, it is the business of one of his associates, who is fond of smoaking, to call at some house, and to request the liberty of lighting his pipe; a denial rarely accompanies such a trifling request, and the stranger is also, of course, often asked to take a chair and to rest himself while he lights his pipe.

An opportunity is then given him to introduce his brethren, who are stationed close to the house, by saying he should be happy to accept of the offer, but that his friends are in waiting for him at the door: an invitation being made to them, the work of salvation commences, by some one of the party looking round to espy if there be any religious books on the tables or desks; in short, few minutes are suffered to elapse, before the subject of religion is started in some way or other, and if these missionaries be favorably heard, the banners of Methodism are soon displayed in the village. A prayer meeting is begun at the house; and the next step in the business of conversion is the appointment of local preachers, whose successes pave the way in due order for the admission of their travelling brethren, when a liberal effusion of the Spirit is the glorious consequence!

The imperfect residence of the established clergy, we are inclined to think, may be safely added to those causes which have contributed in a very considerable degree to the progress of Methodism; but, in laying down this position, let us not be classed among those whose excessive zeal for personal residence has led·them to adopt the erroneous opinion, circulated by the enemies of the church, that the absolute desertion of the clerical office is a thing by no means comparatively rare. That most men, when not resident upon their own livings, are employed as curates to others, every well-informed advocate for the revival of the statute of Henry VIII. must be very ready to acknowledge; but it certainly does not follow, that the clergyman who is connected with his parishioners only by a temporary or precarious tie, does the same good as he who invariably executes the duties of his own parish. The cardinal virtue of residence, if we may so express ourselves, we take then to be, the increase of moral and religious instruction among the lower order of the people, and even the harsh interference of legislative authority may, perhaps, be justified to effect so desirable an end. It must be abundantly clear to all, that resident curates, generally speaking, are not very remarkable for their professional activity: if they regularly perform the ordinary offices of the church, give an hour every Sunday in the year for pulpit exhortations, and answer the common occasional calls of parochial duty, it seldom enters their heads, that they have not discharged all their spiritual functions. The wretched pittance, indeed,

which most of them receive, so ill calculated to maintain even a distant appearance of the state of a gentleman in these expensive times; and the consideration,
that they may toil all their life for the public benefit,
without advancing one step in the ladder of preferment,
are but weak inducements, we must confess, to any gra-
tuitous efforts for the instruction of their fellow creatures: circumstances unquestionably painful and humbling in every point of view to the individuals to whom
they may happen, yet serving forcibly to point out the
necessity of personal residence, for the keeping alive a
due sense of religion in a parish.

Now, on the other hand, a resident incumbent, if
the qualifications of his heart be equal to those of his
head, is naturally impelled, from a variety of motives,
to seek the promotion of the spiritual interest of his
flock by the different means of inspection and remonstrance: the cure of souls with him is a charge of no
small responsibility. The command of St. Paul to
Timothy, to " be instant in season and out of season,"
is constantly fresh in his remembrance: he considers
it, therefore, as essential a part of his duty as preaching, to lose no favourable opportunity of cultivating a
friendly intercourse between himself and those who are
committed to his charge; in order that he may be en-

abled to remedy certain disorders and irregularities, which are of such complexion as cannot be openly redressed; and especially for the sake of acquiring that honourable sort of influence over their minds, which will gradually dispose them to read religious books, to strengthen and enlarge their faith by private and family devotion, and not to forget, in the commerce and business of active life, the unalterable principles of christian charity and love: this, and much more good, will be found on examination to be done by many of our resident parochial clergy; and we may confidently add, that those who possess good means of information respecting that valuable class of men will likewise perceive, that this spiritual acquaintance with their parishioners is not effected by any of those low arts by which the Romish priests obtained such an absolute sway over their laity, and by which the religionists who form the subject of this Essay have such a surprising ascendancy over their followers; but by those free and unconstrained methods, equally suitable to their characters as gentlemen, and to their reputation for learning, common sense, and rational piety*.

* It is the remark of Bishop Watson, whose liberal spirit corresponds with his solid judgment and extensive erudition, that " there are many

Were then the clergy induced to reside in sufficient numbers, not by compulsatory statutes, but by their having proper houses of residence secured to them, through the means of public and private patronage, our church would be fully enabled to resist every open and insidious attack of its enemies, and especially of those sectaries who, unhappily for themselves and the community, have forsaken her sound tenets to embrace others which, while they conspire to puff them up with the vain belief, that to them alone is given the inestimable privilege of discovering the true path of salvation, have no tendency, upon investigation, to render them better men, better christians, or better members of society, than those are, who have not been led, by artful insinuations or audacious invective, to depart from the national religion.

The domestic irreligion of the great is the last of the causes to which may be referred the quick and extensive diffusion of Methodism. That the fundamental principles of christianity are not in general early, strongly, and awfully impressed upon the minds of

among the poorest of the parochial clergy whose merits as scholars, as christians, and as men, would be no disgrace to the most deserving prelate on the bench."—*See his admirable Letter to the Bishop of Canterbury, in* 1783.

the children of the rich, the powerful, and the noble, is a fact as notorious as it is lamentable: and if they are not trained from the tender morn of their infancy to a knowledge of God, and to habits of piety, we cannot reasonably expect to see the precepts of the gospel exemplified in their conduct, upon their attaining the age of manhood. Devoted to pleasure, the love of which, as Aristotle* justly observes, is so nourished up with us from our very childhood, that it is difficult to withdraw the mind from sensual objects, and to fix it upon things remote from sense, they then want the leisure, as much as the ability, to enter into the examination of the eternal truths of the christian religion. Should one of these sons of rank and fashion, on occasion of any great sickness or domestic affliction, reflect with some contrition on his riotous proceedings, that false modesty, or, in other words, that shame which hinders men from doing what they know to be their duty, and the dread of offending against custom, the law of fools, will inevitably suppress the virtuous intention he may have formed of amending his life. On the pagan principle, too, that

* " Ἔτι δὲ ἐκ νηπίου πᾶσιν ἡμῖν συντέθραπται ἡδονή, διὸ καὶ χαλεπὸν ἀποτρίψασθαι τοῦτο τὸ πάθος ἐγκεχρωσμένον τῷ βίῳ."

Ethic. Lib. ii. cap. ii.

the religion of the multitude is entitled to external reverence, he sometimes attends public worship; yet he never hesitates to avow the impious opinion, in the freedom of private conversation, that the christian religion is no more than a system of superstition, invented only to keep the vulgar in obedience, and supported by statesmen for political purposes. In this lamentable ignorance, in this frightful delusion, he probably continues until his " sins are as scarlet;" for if he keeps a mistress, his chaplain, more ambitious of temporal than spiritual honours, and consequently more complacent than sincere, will not dare to tell him that the gospel designates it as whoredom, and that the same unerring book calls his intriguing, adultery, and his duelling, murder.

Now the irreligion of the master is soon communicated to the servant; for there is the same aptness in the latter to adopt the sentiments and principles of the former, as there is to catch and imitate his manners. Is it any wonder, then, that when such a person is led to the Tabernacle by curiosity, the love of novelty, or any other motive, he should imagine himself placed in a new world; should in time mistake the jargon of fanaticism displayed there, for the perfection of real piety; and that, from having no religion at all, he should become so scrupulous and over-righteous, as to doubt if it be not an heinous sin to serve a master whose numerous avocations may sometimes require that he should be inaccessible to visitors when actually at home*? Such is the effect of superiors setting an infamous immoral example to their dependants and inferiors; it either renders them incurably wicked, or transforms them into Methodists†.

From this imperfect but impartial view of the rapid growth of Methodism, it will appear, this pernicious

---

* " A gentleman's servant, who has left a good place because he was ordered to deny his master when actually at home, wishes something on this subject may be introduced into this work, that persons who are in the habit of denying themselves in the above manner may be convinced of its evil."—*See Evangelical Magazine, p. 12.*

† " Persons of *profligate lives* and *libertine sentiments* are wont to take up with such *delusions*. When they are touched with a sense of *guilt*, their reason is so hurried and distracted, that they know not which way to turn, but are apt (like people on some great loss, flying to the conjurer or wizard) to betake themselves to *some fallacious expedients, unsafe security, false doctrine*, or quack remedy, of a mouth that speaketh great things, neglecting every *regular method*. Thus it is no uncommon thing for profligates and libertines, in the *article of danger*, to catch hold on the passport of Popery or Methodism, which probably is a device of satan to beguile them ; or, ' because they have not received the love of truth,' *(2 Thes. chap. ii. v. 9.)* God may permit a strong delusion that they should believe a lie."—*See Enthusiasm of Methodists and Papists compared, Vol. II. p. 157.*

heresy has taken such deep root, that its spreading branches even threaten to overshadow the established church: cottages, huts, woods, moors, and even mines, have been visited by the proselytizing activity of its professors[*]. In the army and navy[+] they have insinuated their doctrines with most unexampled success; and as it is alike indifferent to them whether they accomplish the downfall of our establishment by open violence, or secret stratagem, provided it be accomplished, it is a part of their policy, we understand, to have a large fund for the purchase of livings, to which ministers of their own persuasion are of course always presented. Many wise and pious divines are of opinion, that every sect of christians have their use; inasmuch as, by their means, each important religious truth has the advantage of being set in a full light by some party or other: but surely the propriety of that opinion cannot be admitted respecting a sect

[*] In delineating the particular doctrines of " these self-sent apostles," and in exposing their ambitious hopes, the Bishop of Bangor has indeed justly remarked, that " proselytism, not doctrine, is their great object." P. 19. *See the Charge of this highly esteemed and truly learned Prelate to his Diocese, in* 1808.

[+] For their activity in these two departments of the state, *see the Methodist and Evangelical Magazines.*

which unceasingly labours to blacken and discredit all those who do not adopt its tenets; which, wretchedly destitute of intellectual culture, requires its votaries to be hovering on the precipice of insanity before they can be rightly prepared to come to the *New Birth;* a sect which, without restraint and without remorse, abuses the liberal indulgence of our church, by professing* to belong to it, while it acts in open defiance to all established rules; and lastly, which has impiously dared to confine the future rewards of true piety solely to its own followers.

Of such a sect we shall not be afraid of making this concluding remark, (for never can it become a sincere member of the establishment to be ashamed of publicly contending for orthodoxy from the apprehension of being stigmatized as a bigot,) that while we readily allow the Methodists to be of the most respectable reputations in private society,—as a body, their close hypocricy and fraud, their violent and malignant zeal, their arrogant pretensions to the true character of primitive christians, and their limited

---

* St. Paul assures us, that *Schism is a very dangerous sin;* and as the Methodists seem to entertain a peculiar veneration for that apostle, we may suppose this to be the reason why they still profess *to be* within the pale of the establishment.

notions* of the, mercy of the Almighty, render them
the objects of the pity and contempt of every man of
liberal education and understanding.

* It was from a just dislike to the narrow tenets of Acesius, that the
emperor Constantine desired him to take a ladder, and get up to Heaven
by himself. The ladder of this bishop, we will venture to add, has
been more borrowed by the Methodists, than by any other christian
sect.

ESSAY VII.

ON THE CHARACTER OF THE FINE GENTLEMAN OF THE PRESENT DAY.

IT is worthy of remark, that those who have carried their speculations to the changes of successive ages in manners, dress, and furniture, are prodigal in their censures against the preceding generations in these several particulars: this practice, however, is perhaps one of those that would be more " honoured in the breach than in the observance," notwithstanding the writers of the present day have evinced a most laudable degree of perseverance in praising their own times, and despising those of their fore-fathers: for though any one, after surveying the condition of a savage, may thank that Providence which cast his birth in a period of civilization, yet, for ought we can tell, the formal bow is not a fitter object of derision than the vulgar nod; nor does it appear less difficult to asso-ciate the ideas of elegance and convenience to a velvet suit than a plain broad cloth, or Gothic to Egyptian chairs and footstools.

Fashions, indeed, are as variable as the winds: the writer, therefore, whose patriotism is of that sublime nature, as to prefer his own times to those of any other, will be cautious in commending what is hardly known before it is antiquated: he will rather confine his eulogies to things subject to less sudden and violent revolutions, than decorations in dress and furniture: but even in his view of the present manners, and in the causes alledged for an exclusive admiration of them, we are inclined to suspect, that we shall discover his notions to be more warped by prejudice than directed by reason.

It may be amusing enough to see how far his opinions are founded upon the principle of right reasoning, with respect to the character of the fine gentleman of the present age. In the days of Addison and Pope, an affectation of refinement in his pursuits and pleasures, mixed with a solemn foppery of manners, a style of conversation congenial to camps or courts, with some pretensions to wit and pleasantry, no great antipathy to free-thinkers, a smattering in the polite arts and sciences, a thorough ignorance of foreign states, conjoined however with a decided predilection for every thing *frenchified*, an ineffable contempt for the haters of dancing, music, and fencing, and a behaviour full of politeness, delicacy, and benevolence, towards the female sex,—were held to be the distinguished characteristics of the fine gentleman.

From an indiscriminate application, indeed, of that emphatic term, *fine gentleman*, the word is seldom introduced without being abused. The requisites for obtaining this valuable appellation are so numerous, and placed so much above the common reach, that it is not at all surprising a finished gentleman should be considered as one of those extraordinary characters which are rarely to be met with in real life. Possessed of all those mental attainments which may qualify him to obtain the title of a statesman and scholar, adorned at the same time with that true politeness* and with all those elegant accomplishments which are so seldom united in those who are immersed in trade, or engrossed in study; generous, humane, and courageous, in his disposition; natural, easy, and dignified, in his

---

* True politeness, says an elegant writer, is modest, unpretending, and generous: it appears as little as may be, and when it does, a courtesy would willingly conceal it: it chuses silently to forego its own claims, not officiously to withdraw them: it engages a man to *prefer his neighbour to himself*, because he really esteems him; because he is tender of his reputation; because he thinks it more manly, more *christian*, to descend a little himself, than to degrade another: it respects, in a word, the *credit and estimation* of his neighbour.—*See Sermons preached at Lincoln's Inn, by Bishop Hurd, p.* 172.

manners; carrying the same independent principles into the courts of princes, and the drawing-room of the great, as into the humble cottage; of habits extremely favourable to plain dealing and sincerity; and deeply impressed with the force of moral and religious sentiments; in short, no mean proficiency in every department of excellence;—must be evinced, to justify solid pretensions to the character of a real fine gentleman.

Let us now proceed to state how far the fine gentleman of the present day has benefited from the gifts of philosophy and literature, which have been shed upon him in such great abundance; and in doing this, we must disclaim all idea of turning him into ridicule by an extravagant caricature, or to let the desire of passing for a wit or satyrist overpower our love of truth.

So great a portion of the world aspire to gentility, that it would be now as difficult, as it was before easy, to concentrate their number, when the College of Heralds imposed restraints upon the promiscuous assumption of the title of Esquire*. The hitherto dis-

* Camden, the great antiquary, who was himself a Herald, allows only four sorts of persons to have a legal right to the rank of Esquire: but, according to Sir Edward Coke, every Esquire is a Gentleman, and

tinct orders of nobles and merchants seem now linked together by an indissoluble tie; and, if between their taste in conversation, clothes, and furniture, any difference can be fairly established, it is perhaps to be placed on the monied side; for this sentiment of Horace has never been more completely verified than in the present age: " Nobilitas, sine re, projecta vilior alga." When there are names enrolled in the livery and companies of London, from which the first characters might be justly proud of their descent, we cannot be accused of insinuating in what has just now been said, that those who have sat in the counting-house, or stood in the shop, are not entitled to aspire to the rank of Gentlemen*: on the contrary, it appears to us, that the followers of the mercantile pro-

a Gentleman is defined to be one, " *qui arma gerit*," *who bears coat armour;* which seems to be a strange inaccuracy of distinction in so profound a lawyer. At all events, however, the common opinion, that every Gentleman of landed property who has £300 a year, is an *Esquire*, must be entitled to a place in the catalogue of vulgar errors.

* The original derivation of this word may be evidently traced from the Latin, *gentilis homo*, which was used among the Romans for a race of noble persons of the same name, born of free parents, and whose ancestors had never been slaves, or put to death by law. Thus Cicero, in his *Topica*, " *Gentiles sunt*, qui inter se eodem nomine sunt." " Qui ab ingenuis oriundi sunt." " Quorum majorum nemo servitutem servivit." " Qui capite non diminuti."

fession would have been still more worthy of that respectable name, if so many of them had not been transformed into nabobs and stock-jobbers ; a set of men, of whom it may be truly said, the primary and permanent motives of their indefatigable exertions are an exorbitant love of gain, which, however it may ultimately conduct to a state of independence and elevation, is extremely averse to the acquirements of liberal sentiments and of liberal manners.

> Licet superbus ambulat pecunia
> Fortuna non mutat genus.
>
> *Horace, Ep. Ode ii.*

It would startle the leaders of fashions if we were to compare their occupations to those of the children of Israel ; but it would puzzle many, perhaps, who figure away in a distinguished circle of society, and are intimately acquainted with the habits of what is commonly called the *world*, to find what more they do " than sit to eat, drink, and rise to play*." After having made the grand tour, more like a courier than a traveller, the next step in the career of a fine gentleman is, to commence senator. To expect every man who takes his seat in the House of Lords or Commons should possess eloquence sufficient to maintain

* Exodus, chap. xxxii.

his character as a debater, would be doubtless the acmé of absurdity: but assuredly it is not very unreasonable to require, especially at this momentous crisis, that the young and fashionable mutes of those assemblies should be more conversant in the laws of their country than in those of Newmarket or Brookes's; should sometimes think, that other qualifications are indispensably necessary for the guardians of the lives and liberty of millions, than the skill to play at whist and to calculate the odds. Certainly, in the tremendous situation in which this country is placed, it is no great stretch of indignation to declare, that we cannot even excuse the fine gentleman regarding the senate as a mere coffee-house or place of lounge, however we may overlook his indifference to its important decisions.

Profoundly ignorant as he is in the whole science of politics, in that of dancing, boxing, and driving, he can display a knowledge, zeal, and activity, which entitle him to a character

> " Above all Greek, above all Roman fame."

But a deep, broad, and permanent line of distinction must be drawn between the fine gentleman of that first nation and him of the present day, in the multiplicity of their accomplishments; since, strange to relate, the former had an art of uniting, what the latter has not yet found out even in this age of genius and discovery,—the seemingly repugnant attainments of dancing and philosophy, boxing and poetry, driving and oratory.

Poetry, from time immemorial, has been considered the classical reading of the fine gentleman; but it is very doubtful to us, whether the Sybarite of the present day has any relish for it, at least for its higher flights; since we may fairly presume, that he who proscribes from his table all topics of conversation except those relative to cards, dice, or horse-racing, will more affect the composition of a Little, than a Cowper,—while the pages of such dull and uninformed writers as Hume, Robertson, and Gibbon, should he happen by chance to cast his eye upon them, would be sure to operate upon his spirits as a Sirocco wind*.

The stage is justly regarded as the school of elegant criticism; but according to the canons of haut ton, a tale of sorrow is to produce no other effect upon the

---

* The ennui, if we may be permitted to use this word, with which a Neapolitan is inspired during the continuance of a Sirocco, or south-east wind, is said to be so great as almost to extinguish passion.—*See Brydone's Tour, vol. I. p. 4.* Kotzebue, whose love of paradoxes and singular opinions is as conspicuous as his egotism, affects, in his account of Naples, to find this wind vastly agreeable and invigorating.

fine gentlemen than a sneer of derision, or a complacent survey of the folds of their coats; and by the same wretched perversion of taste and feelings, a coarse joke, or an impertinent piece of buffoonery, is to be applauded till they "almost split the ears of the groundlings."

Politeness, in days of yore, was connected perhaps with too many arts to be graceful or easy; but surely that was preferable to the unbounded freedom of behaviour and kind of determined air now assumed by the fine gentleman. It is but justice, however, to him to admit, that no small share of this change must be attributed to the other sex. There was a time, when a woman of exalted rank would not have mistaken effrontery for dignity, or despised modesty as a vulgar virtue; but now, every thing is sacrificed to the love of notoriety. If then a lady should happen to be offended with some of the *double entendres* which assail her ears from the mouths of these fine gentlemen, or with their impudent air or look, or should take no great liking to hear her best friends pulled to pieces, all of which circumstances we allow are extremely improbable, there is surely no right to complain of an evil which she has so largely contributed to bring about.

The marriage knot is never drawn by the fine gentleman unless to repair his fortunes, Μόνον ἄργυρον βλέπουσι; while all his tenderest sympathies are reserved for his mistress, who constitutes as essential a part of his establishment as his horses and carriages. Acquaintances the fine gentleman has in great abundance, but friends none; for independent of the absurdity of loving an object which we cannot esteem, who would court the affections of so dangerous and capricious a being as a fine gentleman?—since such are the sentiments of honor which his erroneous notions of gentility have instilled into him, that it would be as impossible for him, on any slight or unintentional offence from his friend, to substitute the benevolent delight of forgiveness for the savage glory of aiming a pistol at his head, as it would be for a wild set of visionaries to become at once rational and practical in their schemes of improvement. While he is so completely the child of caprice, that what to-day constituted his chief pleasure, will to-morrow be insupportable and tormenting to him, thus flying from one extreme to another, he exhibits, by turns, all the inconsistencies of human nature. If such be the summer, what must the autumn of a fine gentleman's life disclose?—a hideous void, which cannot be filled up with new pleasures or sensual gratifications, while all those marks of esteem and veneration

> " Which should accompany old age,
> " As honour, love, obedience, troops of friends,
> " He must not look to have; but in their stead,"

the silent contempt and derision of his children and dependants, and the open hatred of all those who are not afraid to practise the most unfashionable virtues in the most fashionable societies.

ESSAY VIII.

ON BASTARDS.

THAT there is a reigning quality in every age, has been demonstrated by the exploring genius of history. If we turn to the annals of antiquity, we shall discover that heroism and cowardice, œconomy and dissipation, have been, by turns, the distinguishing characteristics of the states of Greece and Italy. Much, however, as we are addicted to extol the past at the expence of the present times, the remark may be safely hazarded, that human nature is the same in all ages: the benevolent sentiments of affection and friendship, the angry passions of jealousy and envy, and the detestable ones of malice, hatred, and rage, alike possess the breast of the Hottentot and the European. The character of mankind has, indeed, been always compounded of a mixture of virtues and vices, though at different periods they have appeared under different forms ; but upon the general character of a particular nation, its government unquestionably possesses a considerable influence, since it would be the most striking of all political anomalies, for the rulers of the state to be wise and virtuous, and the people ignorant and profligate.

Every man who has looked upon the late debates in the great council of this nation, will feel no hesitation to avow, that the present age has but small pretensions to that character of devoted patriotism which marked the actions of an early Roman. The sense of a danger, the most unprecedented and unparalleled that ever menaced this country, instead of terminating party dissensions, seems to have rekindled them with greater fury than ever. No, the balance of Europe will sooner be restored, than an union of councils for the public good take place between the leaders of opposition and those of administration.

Some writers have ventured to declare, that selfishness is the ruling principle of this age; others, with more confidence, have affirmed it to be luxury, and have brought forward several instances in support of their peremptory decision; but as it is the part of true wisdom to be careful in erecting general theories on a few particular observations or appearances, we see every reason, from an examination of the particular cases adduced by them, to consider such views as hasty and erroneous, and to concur with those who think that libertinism is the distinguishing characteristic of the present age.

In coinciding, however, with this conclusion, we are fully sensible that it admits of no small modification and restriction ; yet it is certainly to be preferred to those which have determined the character of the present age to be that of selfishness or luxury. Upon the supposition, therefore, that the majority in the low, middle, and high stations of life in this country, are actuated by the dreadful vice of libertinism, (and many facts unfortunately exist to prove, that this hypothesis is founded on the basis of truth,) we are naturally led to the consideration of the peculiar state of those persons denominated Bastards—a theme which may be said to come home to the feelings of almost every man.

According to the calculation of Dr. Colquhoun, in his treatise on Indigence, it appears that the number of persons who are supported wholly or partly by the bounty of others, amounts to more than a million. If this computation be just, and it seems too well founded to excite any suspicion of inaccuracy, we may fairly estimate, that a great part of this melancholy catalogue is swelled by those whose spurious birth deprives them of all rights of society, and upon whose misfortunes, which they owe not to their own follies and vices, but to the crimes of their parents, the most opprobious epithets have been thrown, in almost every nation and every age.

But before we proceed to survey the condition of Bastards, and express our wishes that the legislature would adopt measures that should re-adjust or re-model some of the existing statutes relative to that description of persons, (for assuredly the attempt may be made without infringing upon any of those proud distinctions which are regarded as the appendages of chastity,) a cursory review of the situation of Bastards in ancient times will not perhaps be here misplaced.

From the days of Homer down to the present times, a mark of infamy, more or less, has been affixed upon the issue of concubinage: it is true, indeed, that in the earliest periods, instances have occurred, of natural children being preferred to, or at least being put on an equal footing with, the offspring of marriage; but we may fairly assign the origin of such conduct in the father, to the concubine having taken an entire hold of his affections by her beauty, or an amiable disposition, superior to that of his wife. Under such circumstances we may suppose Telamon to be actuated, when he declared his son Teucer worthy of a seat at his table,

περ εοντα νοθον*, although a Bastard. This solitary example, or even that of natural† children succeeding
to their fathers' kingdoms, in cases chiefly, however,
of failure in legitimate issue, cannot therefore be
urged as a just reason for rejecting the belief of a practice which has been confirmed by the whole course of
antiquity.

If we turn our eyes towards the republics of
Athens and Rome, we shall not fail to discover, that
the laws made against Bastards were well calculated to
inspire the minds of the people with a deep and lasting respect for the institution of marriage. According
to the jurisprudence of Solon, the Athenian Bastard
was declared incapable of assuming the name of his
father, and likewise of inheriting any of his estates,
and was most rigorously excluded from any interference in the affairs of government. Still farther to
widen the distinction between the offspring of the
concubine and that of the wife, it was established by
the same lawgiver, that those who had no legitimate
sons, should be compelled to give their estates to their
daughters: some faint traces, however, of commi-

---

* See Iliad, Lib. viii. line 284.

† In the Odyssey, Ulysses avows himself to be the són of a concubine.
"————εμε δ' αυτη τεκε μητηρ Παλλακις."—Lib: xiv. v. 202.

seration for their condition are discoverable in one of Solon's laws, which allowed them a thousand drachmas, or five Attic pounds. The prototype of this institution may be found in the twenty-fifth chapter of Genesis: " And Abraham gave all that he had unto Isaac ; but unto the sons of the concubines which Abraham had, Abraham gave gifts*." The benevolence and equity of Solon are also equally to be applauded, when he exempted natural children from all obligation to relieve their parents, on the just ground, that not the hope of a progeny, but the indulgence of their sensual passions, was the sole motive which led them to form an illicit+ connection. Instances, however, can be produced where the stern spirit of the law in Athens has been softened in favour of Bastards. It is recorded by Aristotle, in his Politics, that sometimes

---

* *Genesis*, *xxv.* 5, 6.——A Bastard, by the law of Moses, was expelled from the congregation of Israel.—*See Deuteronomy, xxiii.* 2.— When the Judges, however, governed the Israelites, the birth of children who proceeded from unlawful commerce, could not have been looked upon as scandalous: for we read, that Gideon had a son called Abimelech, by a concubine, who had even been his servant, and that this son became king of Sichem after his death.—*Judges, chap. viii. v.* 30, 31.—*chap. ix. v.* 6, 18.—" Non enim vetitus eo tempore concubinatus," observes Grotius on this passage, "neque concubina a matrona, nisi dignitate distabat."

+ See Plutarch, in Solone.

the people admitted these unhappy outcasts into the number of citizens, in order to increase their power in opposition to the great*. And we have a remarkable proof of the ascendancy which that eloquent statesman, Pericles, obtained over the minds of the Athenians, when he could first persuade them to revive the law introduced by Solon, viz. that the rights and honour of a citizen should be exclusively confined to those whose parents had before possessed them, and afterwards, in favour of his own natural children, to cancel it.

Such was the condition of Bastards in the first state of ancient Greece. And if we contemplate the Roman code of laws, the same oppression, the same exclusion from the rights of society, will be found to mark their wretched destiny. Between the tables of Solon, and those of the Decemvirs, some striking similarities may be traced: although, perhaps, in the great and fundamental parts of their system they widely differed. But when Cicero† hesitates not to avow, that the laws of the twelve tables are to be preferred to whole libraries of the philosophers, and affects to

---

* Lib. vi. cap. iv.

† See De Oratore, Lib. i. and De Legibus, Lib. ii.

contemn the Athenian legislator, it might be reasonably expected, that *the rule of right*, and *the fountain
of all public and private justice*, for so those tables are
styled by Tacitus* and Livy+ should contain some
positive injunctions, which fixed the condition of Bastards in the scale of political beings; but no such trait
of justice appears upon the face of them. The son of
a prostitute, says the law, is to be excluded from the
rights of the people‡. The only act of benevolence
which extended towards his state, and this is destitute
of all pretensions to originality, if we may credit the
story§ of the tables of the Decemvirs being borrowed
from the laws of Solon, is that which bears an exact
affinity to a former quoted maxim of Grecian jurispru-

* Annalia, Lib. iii. cap. xxviii.

+ Hist. Rom. Lib. iii. cap. xxxiv.

‡ Ex meretrice natus, ne concionetur.—*Quintilian, Lib. viii.* The
reader must not here confound the son of the concubine with that of the
prostitute; since the former might be legitimated, and succeed to the
sixth part of the inheritance of his putative father. This commerce
was therefore deemed an inferior sort of marriage.

§ Livy believes that three distinguished personages visited Athens,
under the administration of Pericles, for the abovementioned purpose.—
*Hist. Rom. Lib. viii. See the satisfactory reasons assigned by Gibbon
for rejecting this embassy. The Decline and Fall of the Roman Empire, Vol. VIII. p. 8, 9.*

dence, namely, that the Bastard shall not be obliged to toil for the subsistence of his uncertain father. It is, however, incumbent upon us to add, that although the old Roman laws shewed no favour to natural children, in the reign of Valentian I. a father was permitted to leave a small part of his fortune to his natural children, and that this indulgence was confirmed by the humanity and justice of Theodosius the younger*.

Quitting these periods of antiquity, and descending to the middle ages, we shall discover that the manners of those times were far more favourable to the condition of Bastards. In the eleventh and fourteenth centuries, the spurious race of adultery and prostitution is to be seen not only enjoying the honours and offices of public life, but even obtaining the sway of kingdoms. To confirm this last assertion, it is sufficient to cite the names of William† the Conqueror, and Henry of Transtamare, and John grand master of the order of Avis; nor did England, Castile, or Portugal, ever attempt to dethrone these monarchs on the principle of their illegitimate births. But the most

* See Gothofred ad Cod. Theod. Lib. iv. tit. vi. *p.* 351, &c.

† The letters patent granted by William the Conqueror to Alain Count of Brittany begin thus, Ego Willielmus cognomento Bastardus.—*See Du Cange Gloss. Lat. tit. i. p.* 502.

remarkable instances appear in the Italian states in the fifteenth and sixteenth centuries, where the distinction seems to have been wholly dispensed with. In 1450 Borso d'Este, although illegitimate, succeeded his brother, the famous Lionello, in the government of Ferrara, to the exclusion of Hercules and Sigismund his legitimate brothers. Alfonso king of Naples was succeeded in that government in 1468 by his illegitimate son Ferdinand I. although his brother John, king of Navarre, succeeded him in his Sicilian and Spanish dominions. In Florence the government was assumed in 1530 by Alexander dé Medici, who being himself of illegitimate birth, married Margaret the natural daughter of Charles V.; and she having survived her husband, was afterwards married to Octavio Farnese the illegitimate son of Paul III. after whose death she became governess of the Low Countries, and discharged that important trust with distinguished ability. Notwithstanding the plausible efforts made to prove the legitimacy of Clement VII. in order to qualify him to assume the tiara, he was unquestionably of illegitimate birth; and we are expressly told by one of the Italian historians, that it was considered in those times as no disgrace for a Pope to have Bastard children, and to endeavour by every method to render them rich and powerful; but that on the contrary, such Pontiffs were considered as judicious and able men*. " Blest be the Bastard's birth," was an exclamation which the poet might then have made use of, and found it sanctioned by the truth of history : but though the moralist may lament the fate of those who are deprived of their common rights for crimes not their own, and rejoice when they are restored to them, he would not wish to extend the clemency of the laws so far as to recognize the Bastard's right of succession to the crown; since no maxim of modern policy is more incontrovertible, than that the title of a sovereign cannot be too clear, nor his birth too much respected; for with them the peace and welfare of future generations are deeply connected.

In England, however, every condition seems to be introduced by the municipal law, that could render the institution of marriage dignified and venerable ; for it deemed all those to be Bastards who were born before wedlock. The civil and canon laws were more indulgent to the frailty of human nature, and acknowledged the legitimacy of the child on the nuptials of his parents. When the bishops, in the parliament assembled at Merton, in the twentieth year of the

* See Bernardo Segni, Lib. viii.

reign of Henry III, proposed to the earls and barons, that children born before marriage should be esteemed legitimate, in conformity to the canon law, the unanimous reply was, *We will not change the laws of England, which have been hitherto used and approved**. It is, however, reasonable to suppose, that the peers would not so hastily have pronounced a law which throws all the punishment upon the descendant of an unlawful connexion, if the bishops, under the protection of their spiritual leader, the Roman Pontiff, had not made in that reign several great and effectual efforts to establish the canon, upon the ruins of the common law of the kingdom. They wisely, therefore, determined to embrace the first favourable incident of setting proper bounds to an attempt so injurious to their own and the common interests.

By the Germans, many of whose usages and political institutions have been adopted by us, the unhappy Bastard was scarcely ranked among the human species; but in Spain and France he participated in almost all the rights of society, and was in some

* Et omnes barones unâ voce responderunt, quod nolunt leges Angliæ mutare, quæ huc usque usitatæ sunt et approbatæ.—*See Statute of Merton*, 20 *Hen. III. Chap. ir.;* and also *Coke upon Littleton, Lib. iii. Cap. vi. Sect.* 40.

respects upon a footing with legitimate children. During the first and second races of the kings of France, if a prince or noble acknowledged a natural child to be his child, this simple confession was deemed equivalent to any formal legitimation; but the tyrannous inequality of the law condemned the Bastards of an inferior station to a perpetual slavery or villainage. After the succession of the Capetian line, the royal Bastards were, however, no longer suffered to exalt their heads above the level of their fellow-subjects; they were no longer held to be of the blood royal, and every extraordinary dignity was refused them, except that of bearing the arms of France with a bar. A similar limitation of honours took place with regard to the Bastards of princes and nobles: by an ordinance of the year 1600, it was established, that the natural children of nobility should not be admitted into the class of gentlemen, unless they obtained letters of nobility. A more fortunate revolution attended the plebeian Bastards; by the law of that enlightened period, they were no longer confounded with the rest of the cattle on the domains of their masters, but began to be considered in the respectable light of freemen; and if we except the power of receiving and transmitting succession, it will be difficult to mention any privilege which they did not enjoy with the rest of their fellow subjects*.

Having now glanced at the laws which reason, and prejudice more powerful than reason, enacted against the name† and condition of Bastards in ancient periods, we shall proceed to consider the present rights, or perhaps more properly speaking, the incapacities of those who have that stain affixed upon their birth in this country, and the duties which the law imposes upon the authors of their existence. The jurisprudence of England, as we have before remarked, brands him with the name of Bastard who is not born in lawful wedlock: if marriage, however, takes place within a few months of the delivery of the child, the law is not so rigorous as to refuse to it the rights of legiti-

* See Œuvres de Chancelier d'Aguesseau, Tom. vii. p. 881.

† " In English, hee is called *base borne*, and thereupon some say, that a *Bastard* is as much as to say, *one that is a base naturall;* for *aerd* signifieth nature."—*See Coke upon Littleton, vol. II. lib. iii. c.* 6, 244 *a.* But Sir Henry Spelman is dissatisfied with this derivation, and considers it as a pure Saxon word, *Bastardt*, viz. impure natus, ut apud nos, *upstart* dicitur homo novus.—*See Spelman's Gloss.*—Bastardt. There is, however, great speciousness in some writers supposing the word Bastard was derived from *base-terred*, or laid on the ground; because such illegitimate offspring were not entitled to the honours of filiation till by the father taken up from the ground: this ceremony was called in Latin, *tollere*, after which the child was considered little, if at all, inferior to what is now understood by lawfully begotten.

macy; although it was ordained, that if the marriage happened subsequent to the conception of the child, it should suffer the disgrace of bastardy. The rights, if we may use that word in speaking of these outcasts of society, are so few, that they may be soon enumerated. Regarded in the eye of the law as the son of nobody, the Bastard is declared incapable of inheritance and succession; but although he is not called to the inheritance of any possessions, it does appear that the law authorizes him to gain a surname by reputation*.

It is the evident object of the legislature to have perfect justice dealt out alike to all; and although this is never attainable, from the utter impossibility of civil laws to ascertain the punishment due to him, for instance, who commits the crime of ingratitude†, with a degree of sufficient accuracy to satisfy the feelings of the injured party, nevertheless, to keep it constantly in view, ought to be the fundamental principle of every code; it may therefore be reckoned a rare

---

* See Blackstone's Commentaries, vol. I. p. 459.

† There was a law in Athens to prosecute those for ingratitude who did not return kindnesses.—*See Potter's Antiquities of Greece, vol. I. p. 170.* How apparent is the utility of such a law, but how impracticable its execution!

species of injustice to deny the Bastard the rights of society, and yet to fetter him with the same restrictions in the disposal of his person as the law imposes on all legitimate children; and this is done, when it declares, that if a Bastard marries under age by licence, he must obtain the consent of his reputed father, guardian, or mother*.

Of the incapacities of the Bastard, the principal one may be said to consist in being ordained the heir to no one, and likewise of being incapable of having any heirs, but those of his own body; for as he is stigmatized by the law with the degrading appellation of *filius nullius*, and sometimes *filius populi*, he can have no legal ancestors, and of consequence none can be entitled to succeed to his vacant possessions but those who claim a lineal descent from him: but the civil law differs essentially in this point, and grants to a Bastard the right of inheritance, if after his birth the mother was married to the father. It still further proclaims its humanity and justice, when it declares, that if the father has no lawful wife, and if the concubine was never married to the father, yet she and her bastard son should both be admitted each to one-twelfth of the inheritance: nor does it expose the Bastard to any

* See Blackstone's Commentaries, vol. I. p. 458, note 11.

legal disqualification of possessing the whole of his mother's estate, although she was never married ; an indulgence which was founded on the principle of there being no difficulty in ascertaining who was his mother, whatever there might be in ascertaining his father*. But for what reason the civil law should prohibit the Bastard from receiving even a gift+ from his father in some cases, is a question which we leave to be resolved by those who are more conversant in those nice distinctions, so often made by law equity, to the total overthrow of common sense.

In viewing then the municipal law of the kingdom, and the civil law in regard to Bastards, it is evident, from the differences already enumerated, that their chief outlines by no means concur; and it must be confessed, that the latter seems much more disposed than the former to remove the badge of infamy from that unhappy portion of the human species. The only decisive instance where our law abates its severe tyranny against the Bastard, and seems to befriend him, is, when a man has two sons, the elder of whom is a natural, and the other a legitimate child: it then enacts, that if the father die, and the Bastard enter

* See Blackstone's Commentaries, vol. II. p. 247.
+ See Code, 6, 5, 7, 5.

upon his lands and enjoy them to his death, they shall descend by inheritance to his issue, to the utter exclusion of the legitimate son and his heirs; because it is not just, observes that great oracle of jurisprudence, Lord Coke, for a man to be bastardized after his death who has passed for legitimate the whole time of his life*: but this rule is applicable only when a man has a bastard son, and afterwards marries the mother, by whom he has a legitimate son. This order of succession, though regulated by nature, was established as a punishment to the mother, for her negligence in not dispossessing the Bastard during his life time; nor would the law give validity to the title of any other kind of Bastard. Some trivial indulgence our law also shews to the Bastard in the transmission of his property: it was formerly decided, that if he died intestate, and without wife or progeny, the ordinary might dispose of his goods *in pios usus :* but under those existing circumstances it was considered, that the king was entitled to his private property as administrator; and it was customary for the crown to grant the administration of it to some of the relations of the Bastard's father

---

* Justum non est aliquem post mortem suam facere bastardum, qui toto tempore vita sua pro legitimo habebatur.—*See Coke upon Littleton, vol. II.* 24 *a.*

or mother, reserving one-tenth or some small proportion of it*. Such are the incapacities of the Bastard;
and if we add to the list, that equity will not supply
the defect of a surrender of a copyhold to a natural,
as it will to a legitimate child, it must be obvious to
every one, that the legislature has scrupulously guarded
against the admission of Bastards into the rights of
society.

It would now be the most pleasing part of the Essay
to represent the law, though hostile to the political
existence of the Bastard, laying its parents under
an obligation to continue their support, until he had
some certain means of succeeding in the world: but
the more agreeable is the fiction, the more intolerable
becomes the reality. By the cruel equality of the law,
for well does it deserve to be called so in this case, the
rich parent is not obliged to make a greater provision
than the poor one for the natural issue of his body†.
It follows, therefore, that however qualified a Bastard
may be by his talents, for stations of respectability and
consequence, unless his opulent father be so far
awakened to the sensibilities of nature, as to remove

* See Blackstone's Commentaries, vol. II. p. 506, note 9.

† See Burn's Ecclesiastical Law, vol. I. p. 132, note 5.

those checks and impediments which hinder his promotion, the abilities which he possesses may be considered as so many curses. Between the Bastard of the gentleman and of the peasant, we do then contend, that a wise legislature should enforce some distinction; and not deny to the former the opportunity of reaping some substantial advantage from his superior education; which is effectually done, if, in a fit of caprice, prejudice, or passion, the father should withhold that support which, continued to a proper season, would have enabled his natural son to obtain that situation for which he had been so long labouring: since the fact is notorious, that there are those, who reflect as little on leaving a natural child to depend entirely upon himself, and his own bodily and intellectual energies, as the Turkish Emperor would do on exercising his privilege of killing fourteen men a day without assigning any reason.

We trust, the remarks we have already made will be sufficient to demonstrate, that the Bastard has no very powerful inducement to join in the general praise of the unexampled impartiality and benevolence of our laws. It is not even a paradox, perhaps, to say, that the evils of a despotic are to be preferred by him to the blessings of a free government; for which is the more mortifying,—to live under a government clogged with a multiplicity of restrictions and severities, and where the name of liberty cannot be mentioned without the greatest peril, but to which he is not more exposed than the rest of the community; or, to be fixed in a free state, but to see its inestimable privileges and advantages, as far as respects himself, rendered inoperative? This question, we should suppose, needs only to be stated to be decided: and admitting the position, that the Bastard has just ground to complain of the disabilities and incapacities under which he labours, it remains for us to consider the reasonableness and expediency of relaxing them.

They who refuse their consent to improvements, from an overstrained dread of innovation, will shut their ears to all arguments which can be advanced for the removal of the various privations of the Bastard; and will be disposed to view those who propose them in the light of political theorists, who are perpetually opposing crude and hasty conclusions to the unerring deductions of experience. Such men, indeed, allow their feelings of humanity to be so completely stifled by the abhorrence of innovation*, that with them, this is a

* To persons of this description the words of Canuleius are peculiarly applicable.—" Can no circumstances authorize innovations? and must

question which has no connection with any practical
and moral purposes; or else, so perverted are their
judgments by their ill-founded fears, that they would
only class it with those which are productive of the
most mischievous consequences. Not so do the advo-
cates of a more wise, just, and liberal policy, reason
and determine; though it is the peculiar property and
distinguishing characteristic of laws to be deaf to every
voice but that of the public benefit, yet to throw upon
a particular class of beings all its weights, and none of
its benefits, appears to them to be both unwise and unjust: it likewise seems to them reasonable to maintain,
that our laws, in not paying any attention to the wants
and feelings of Bastards, have obstructed rather than
promoted the great cause of virtue and morality; for
as their race, from the licentiousness of the times, is
unfortunately so numerous as to comprehend a very
considerable portion of the community, no pains
should be spared, no incentives be wanted, to render
them respectable members of the state. At present
they are considered as little better than the scum or
off-scouring of society; but if parliament, in its om-
nipotence, would frame a statute, which would give

those things which have utility for their object not be done because they
have never been done before ?"—*See Titus Livius, Lib. iv. cap. iv.*

natural children a legal claim on the property of their parents, it would pave the way to make them better men and better citizens, and would ultimately check or suppress those habits which are abhorrent from the inflexible rules of virtue prescribed by the laws for the good of society; nor does the recollection, that if such a measure were to receive the sanction of a law, how much it would intrench upon the temporal advantages of legitimate children, at all abate their desire of seeing it brought to pass, since, in the fulness of their benevolence, the above class of political reasoners maintain, that the evil experienced thereby would not be commensurate to the great and permanent good thus likely to be effected.

Such, we believe, are the leading arguments of these philanthropists. It is pretty evident that the legislature has imposed such restrictions on the Bastard as are subversive of a spirit of a just and social pride and of improvement among them; and it may likewise perhaps be rationally suspected, that these restrictions are repugnant to the genius of a constitution which is ever disposed to reverence the principles of justice and humanity: but as the most plausible theories, when reduced to practice, are often attended with the most futile or pernicious consequences, it may be questioned whether the evil resulting from an encroachment on the pecuniary rights of the Bastard could counterbalance the good which a mitigation of the statute against him might produce. Those who, in their blind admiration of the ancient code of jurisprudence, are led to shrink from every proposal of reformation as wild and dangerous, or to ridicule it as visionary and absurd, most zealously contend, that the laws in respect to Bastards, from the circumstances in which they were formed, were entitled to be immortal, and boldly challenge their opponents to bring forth an instance of a Bastard being legitimated by an act of parliament, bating the exception of John of Gaunt's children.

But the British constitution has experienced a mighty revolution since the days of King Richard the Second. The enlightened statesman of the present day, however strong a predilection he may entertain for a system, the benefits of which have been so well ascertained by experience, yet if some errors and inconveniences, hardships and oppressions, are discoverable in certain parts of it, his respect for that ancient system will not carry him so far as to oppose such remedies as sound policy and practical humanity shall suggest for their rectification: besides, we may venture to ask these fierce and determined foes to innovation, how comes it, if all the laws in respect to the Bastard are meant to be immortal, that the one which declared him incapable of taking holy orders, though that was afterwards dispensed with, yet rigorously excluded him from becoming a dignitary of the church, should now have slept for ages?

If then, in times less favourable to the feelings of justice and humanity, it was not deemed a sacrilege to abolish or render obsolete some decisions relative to the Bastard, it will not perhaps be considered in the light of an objectionable position, even to those who manifest the most inveterate dislike to proffered improvements, to advance, that the modification of the laws in force against Bastards would stop up many avenues to abandoned wickedness and profligacy; would much contribute to check that growing levity and dissipation of mind which are the greatest impediments to all substantial improvements in virtue and goodness; and lastly, would promote the developement of the moral energies among those whom the legislature has only noticed in such a manner, as if their habits, affections, and system of manners, were as offensive as their condition is degrading and deplorable. In Denmark, whose despotic structure of government promises but little respect to the rights of those who are doomed to perpetual ignominy by the most enlightened of all political constitutions, to its eternal honour be it spoken, it is decreed, that natural children should have half the property which the law allows to legitimate children, and the whole if there are no legitimate children*. May we not then indulge the pleasing hope, that the period is not far distant, when the august bodies, in whose hands is deposited the legislative authority, will, without losing sight of the land-marks which our forefathers have set, deem it as unwise, as it certainly is unjust, to defraud of all political rights a set of beings, who seem hitherto fated to complain of grievances, which become more galling from being unpitied, more intolerable from being unmerited.

* See Cattau, Tableau des Etats Danois.

ESSAY IX.

ON THE QUALIFICATIONS REQUISITE IN AN AMBASSADOR.

THAT the French have not only become masters of the destiny of their neighbours, but even established themselves in universal power, as much by the effects of intrigues as by the force of arms, is one of those propositions which needs only to be stated in order to be fully admitted; and we are afraid it is not less abundantly clear, that we have as much augmented the resources and dominions of France, and completed the ruin of our allies, by the conduct of our diplomatic affairs, as that we are still able to baffle and defy all the attacks of that overgrown power chiefly, or rather solely, by the means of our naval greatness.

It would certainly therefore be no very great absurdity of reasoning to conclude, that as it is a distinguishing feature of the policy of France, in respect to her foreign relations, to employ none but men of the most manageable and imposing characters, the expediency of England exercising an equally vigilant anxiety in the appointment of its ambassadors, would be obvious even to those who are but superficially acquainted with this most important branch of politics. Yet, if we look with an impartial eye to the history of our late continental wars, the events and termination of them will but too forcibly demonstrate, that no such vigilant anxiety was displayed for the general good of the community.

As it is then an established opinion, that able men in this country, with but very few exceptions, have not been of late years nominated to diplomatic stations, to which circumstance we presume a great portion of the late and present miseries of Europe may be safely traced, the attempt in us may be pardoned to exhibit a short sketch of those parts, natural and acquired, which we humbly conceive are indispensably necessary for the representatives of our sovereign to possess, in order that they may be qualified to discharge their high functions with credit to themselves and honor to their country. An enquiry into the causes which have led to that ignorance so manifest and so deplorable in our foreign policy, would doubtless be more curious and interesting than the picture we are about to present to our readers; yet it will be assuredly recollected, that any such enquiry, even if it were conducted with all possible decorum, would inevitably entangle us in discussions of too personal a nature, to be touched, much less to be dwelt upon in the form of a sober and dispassionate essay.

From the vast range of knowledge necessarily embraced by the science of politics, we should be justified in considering, that no one could expect to make any great proficiency, unless he brought to it a considerable portion of inquisitiveness, understanding, and discernment. Yet it is worthy of observation, that in no study have we more smatterers and fewer adepts. This observation may particularly apply to our diplomatists in general. In those days when France was only counted among the great powers of the continent, without possessing the least ascendancy over them, it was customary for those who were enrolled in the diplomatic corps, first to become pupils before they aspired to be masters. But when France began to swallow up every other state that it could bring within its grasp, by a singular defect of foresight, we seemed more supine than ever in guarding against the return of past evils, by not taking care to meet its ambitious despot with his own arts, and to fight him with his own weapons ; or, in other words, to remove all inferior men from their diplomatic stations.

Some persons we know, and sensible ones too in other respects, have persuaded themselves, that a natural sagacity and a good reasonable judgment, are qualifications sufficient for the post of an ambassador. Possessed of these, he may step forth, they think, like Minerva from the brain of Jove, all provided to become a fit representative of his sovereign. But those who are disposed to embrace this opinion take little or no account of the retrospect and comparison which is necessary to be made in all political matters, in order to acquire that reasonable good judgment, or of the infinite modifications and new combinations it is capable of undergoing. In this assertion we would not be understood as saying, that no man can execute the office of an envoy with success, unless he early discover that decided predilection for it which Pascal did for mathematics and Vandyke for painting. All we profess to urge is, that he would assuredly expose his ignorance and presumption, who should imagine, that the duties of an ambassador* are to be properly discharged, and

---

* They who are curious about the primitive origin of terms, will not perhaps think the following note to be impertinent. In the acts of the 5th general council, the *Apocrisarius* of the monastery of Mount Sinai, a sort of resident in the imperial city in the name of foreign churches and bishops, is called by the Latin translator, *Ambassiator;* and Suicer observes, in his Thesaurus Ecclesiasticus, *tom. I. p.* 456, that in pro-

the dignity of his station preserved, without his displaying that enlargement and expansion of intellect, and acuteness of discrimination, which can only be the result of having first read and travelled much, in his closet, and afterwards looked upon men and affairs in a variety of countries and a variety of views.

Before any one can reasonably hope to be distinguished as a diplomatist, or even venture to assume the character of one, he should first judge it expedient to visit the principal courts of Europe, in order to inform himself, as far as lies in his power, of all those circumstances which may hereafter enable him to transact the affairs of his own country with the best possible advantage. Nor is it unimportant to remark, that in this private situation he will stand the fairest chance of getting rid of those vulgar misconceptions and local prejudices, which if he suffer to regulate or influence his official conduct, and this has been of late too often the case, will produce consequences more untoward from being unexpected, and which cannot afterwards be averted by the wisest plans or the deepest stratagems.

It would be a rare species of absurdity to imagine an ambassador ignorant of the language of the country

cess of time the Emperors gave the name Apocrisarii to their own ambassadors, and it became the common appellation of every sort of legate.

to which he was dispatched; yet a certain appointment has not put this supposition beyond the bounds of credibility. Upon such an appointment, however, no censure can be too great; for occasions will daily and hourly occur in the course of an embassy, where, if the head of it does not display the minutest accuracy, both in conversing and writing, the interests of his country may be materially affected. If we attend also to the opinions of those who are not disposed to see the urgent necessity of an ambassador's possessing intellectual attainments of the highest order, it will appear, that our regret need not be very excessive, if the stock of his historical information be but scanty and imperfect. We are, however, led to believe, that reasoning to be fundamentally erroneous, which teaches us to think, that because in this critical state of public affairs events have arisen of a nature so totally new and unlooked for, as to appear without a precedent in the page of ancient or modern history, the study of it is not calculated to fit a man in an eminent degree for the office or business of an ambassador. In tracing the springs of human conduct, that knowledge of the world which is communicated by experience, will perhaps in many cases enable us to form a more successful judgment, than that which is derivable from

history and books of speculation: yet it is equally undeniable, that he who has been accustomed to contemplate with a philosophic eye the fortunes of nations
and the revolutions of empires, which history exhibits
in successive order, will oftentimes act in transactions
of the highest import, with a promptitude, decision,
and success, which will be set down by the ignorance
of spectators as the effects of good fortune, instead of
being ascribed to the excellence of that study which
teaches us to foresee events, and of course to be prepared
for them. As well therefore may it be said, that active
life is not the noblest sphere of a great genius, as that
a thorough acquaintance with modern history must not
be enumerated among the primary acquirements of
him, who aspires to pass the chief part of his life in important embassies. But whatever difference of opinion
may subsist upon this assertion, we will venture to affirm, the following will meet the approbation of all
classes of politicians: that no prospect of present or
future advantage should induce any one to go as an ambassador to a country, for whose character, taste, or
manners, he professes to entertain the sentiments of
aversion or contempt. Nor does the possibility of those
sentiments being either just or laudable, at all compen-
sate for the existence of this evil. The whole train of

national and domestic prejudices, and the antipathies
which they inspire, ought to be banished from the recollection of the foreign minister; or else his influence
will be remote or feeble, in contributing to the honor
and interest of his particular nation, and to the happiness of Europe at large.   Far be it from us in this assertion to insinuate aught personally disrespectful of
those who have of late years been employed in our foreign diplomacy; although we shall never cease to contend, that he does but half discharge his duty as an ambassador, who neglects the opportunity which his local
situation affords him, of taking a near view of the intrigues of contending factions, by mixing indiscriminately with the heads of them, and thus of turning
their mutual jealousies and dissensions to the benefit
of his own country*.   It was usual in the diplomacy

* Whitelocke, in enumerating the duties of an ambassador, observes,
that among many other things, " he is also to inform himself of the face
and government of the country to which he is sent ; the avenues by sea
and land ; where it is strong, where it is weak ; where dangerous to an
enemy ; what fortifications it hath by art or nature ; what the laws and
privileges of the people are ; what the trade is; what their militia, their
revenue and taxes, whether grievous ; what the affections of the people,
what factions of the multitude or great men, whether upon grounds of
rule or religion ; what their foreign leagues are ; whether their councils
depend only upon the Prince or the state of the country.   And herein
he must be wary, lest he cause jealousy of his diving into the secrets of
another; but he must commend what is commendable, and create a belief

of the court of Louis XV. to employ an unaccredited agent, whose reports were a check upon the actual ambassador. Many good effects perhaps would be produced by such a system of diplomacy being adopted in this country.

With more malice than truth we hope it has been asserted, that our ambassadors shut themselves up as closely in their hotels as the Grand Sultan does in his seraglio. Were this assertion true in its utmost latitude, the causes of the French influence, in almost every court on the Continent, prior to its subjugation, might be easily inferred: for if a person were ever so eminent in the talents fit for a diplomatic situation, but so immured himself, his views would necessarily be bounded to a narrow focus, compared with him who made it his chief business to be equally acquainted with the genuine passions, interests, and desires of the favorites of the people of the crown. In some cases, " fas est ab hoste doceri." Had we then condescended to imitate France in her policy of only calling the ablest of her subjects to the post of ambassadors, a policy so obvious as to have been adopted even in her revolutionary days, and since brought to such fatal

of his good wishes and affections to them."—For this sensible passage, *see the appendix to his Journal of the Swedish Embassy, vol. II, p. 459.*

perfection, craft would have been opposed to craft, zeal to zeal, which would have been the only sure way of correcting that turbulent, daring, and wicked spirit, which has rent asunder the contexture of almost every state.

But interest, and not superior merit, is the most efficacious recommendation with us, alike to foreign and domestic posts of great responsibility and honor: until therefore a complete reform be made in that particular, we may look in vain, in the conduct of our affairs abroad, for sagacity in forming plans, firmness in executing them, boldness in encountering difficulties, presence of mind in improving every occasional advantage, and for that cool intrepidity which cannot be diverted from steadfastly adhering to its object by any sally of passion, however sudden and extravagant*.

* To establish the Pretender upon the throne of England, Cardinal Alberoni meditated the design of engaging the Czar and the King of Sweden in a war with that country; and when the famous Lord Harrington carried to him a list of ships then lying before Barcelona, which were to act against it if he persisted in his attempt of embroiling the peace of Europe, the rage of Alberoni was so excessive, that he snatched the paper from the hands of the ambassador, and tore it into a thousand pieces. Not the least disconcerted by this unexpected act, Lord Harrington calmly proceeded with the thread of his discourse, *et comme je sois, Monseigneur.*—For this anecdote, *see Memoires du Cardinal Alberoni, p. 96.* Such deliberate coolness is deserving of praise and imitation, for oftentimes the safety and welfare of nations depend upon it.

In lieu of these qualities we shall be certain, however, of finding a hesitating, formal, and official spirit, which, while others are acting, is deliberating; and conceives that the vital interests of a nation are best studied and advanced by a scrupulous attention to those ceremonials, which, to use the emphatic words of Sir William Temple, himself a master of the diplomatic science, " seems to have been only raised and cultivated by those men, who wanting other talents to value themselves in the employments of ambassadors, endeavoured to do it by exactness or nicety in the forms*." Now such punctillios in their consequences remind us forcibly of the old tactics, by which the Prussians confidently imagined they should beat the French; but before the former had even performed one of their tardy evolutions, the quickness and energy of the latter had enabled them to discharge their pieces, and rout their ranks.

Co-existent with such predilection for stiff etiquette, or rather arising out of it, is a disposition so proud and unbending as even to indispose those against us, who might else be inclined, from disappointment, hatred, or other motives, to espouse our interests in the most open and cordial manner. The necessity in-

* See Temple's Works, vol. II. p. 387.

deed of a negociator professing conciliating qualities in critical and delicate missions, has been lately so deeply felt, that it is impossible to enumerate the evils which have been occasioned to all Europe for the want of them. No man perhaps better understood or practised the rare art of living with his enemies, in such a way, as if they were one day to be his friends, than the celebrated Lord Chesterfield : in this respect, as in many others, his diplomatic career may be quoted as a model for those who profess to think, that the terms *conciliating* and *dignified* are utterly irreconcileable; and how subservient to the interests of his country he made those feelings, and that language of conciliation, which he uniformly evinced towards his public foes, may be partly attested by the following passage, which, though long, is too important to be mutilated :—

" Abbé de la Ville had abilities, temper, and industry. We could not visit, our two masters being at war; but the first time I met him at a place, I got somebody to present me to him; and I told him, that though we were to be national enemies, I flattered myself we might, however, be personal friends. Two days afterwards I went early to solicit the deputies of Amsterdam, where I found Abbé de la Ville, who had been beforehand with me; upon which I addressed myself to the deputies, and said smilingly, I am very sorry, gentlemen, to find my enemy with you; my knowledge of his capacity is already sufficient to fear him; we are not upon equal terms, but I trust to your own interests against his talents; if I have not had this day the first word, I shall at least have the last. They smiled: the Abbé was pleased with the compliment, and the manner of it. He stayed about a quarter of an hour, and then left me to my deputies, with whom I continued upon the same tone, though in a very serious manner. I told them that I was only come to state their own true interests to them plainly and simply, without any of those arts which it was necessary for my friend to make use of to deceive them. I carried my point, and continued my *procédé* with the Abbé, and by this easy and polite commerce with him, at third places, I often found means to fish out from him whereabouts he was*."

Another evil, of no small magnitude, also arising from an ambassador's accustoming himself to unsocial habits, and to an unbending and unaccommodating tone, is the following:—If he entertains a suspicion that some secret league is in agitation, to which

* See Lord Chesterfield's Letters to his Son, Letter 258.

he is not allowed to be privy, from some of its operations being detrimental to the interests of his own country, no other chance is presented to him of discovering it, than that of offering a large bribe to some underling of the court, whose profession is perfidy, and who in the end proves to be as absolute a stranger to the league in question, and to the characters of the actors in it, as the ambassador himself. Now assuredly this is a most weak, clumsy, and ruinous mode of proceeding: far better would it be, in our humble judgment, for this legal spy, a term which, however humiliating, may yet be applied with the strictest propriety to the functions of an ambassador, to invite the most eminent persons of opposite political interests to his table, where, if he exemplified in his behaviour the famous Italian precept, *volti sciolti et pensieri stretti*, it is more than conjectural that, in the freedom of intimacy, and in the hilarity of social enjoyment, he would succeed in drawing from some one of his guests that sort of authentic information which would either satisfy him, that his suspicions of a league being formed against his court were without any trace of foundation, or else enable him to take such measures as would counteract the effects of it. Such craft, if carried into the intercourse of private life, would doubtless entitle those who practised it to the severest reprobation; but, in diplomatic transactions, we are to conclude it is amply justified by the principles of state reason, since personages* have not disdained to resort to it, who, in all other occurrences, manifested a strong repugnance to the arts of dissimulation.

The Athenians forbade that the names of Harmodius and Aristogiton, who had delivered their country from the tyranny of Hippias and Hipparchus, should ever be given to slaves. If our legislature had decreed, at the commencement of the French revolution, that none should receive pensions for their diplomatic services but those whose merits in that department were publicly acknowledged by our enemies, we have no doubt that the ambassadors of this country would have made a greater figure in the eyes of Europe than they have done for these last ten years.

* Sir William Temple *(see his Works, vol. I. p. 266)* and Lord Horatio Walpole *(see Coxe's Memoirs of that Nobleman, p. 465)* have both conceived, that the best intelligence was to be obtained in the convivial intercourse of the table; and though the latter was a most rigid economist, yet for that purpose the same table was always kept in his absence by his secretary.—We have been informed, as an indisputable fact, that an application which a certain ambassador made in the morning to Talleyrand, was in the evening granted to his secretary, whose good fortune it was to meet him at a friend's house, and who, in the freedom of familiar conversation, had the skill to seize the favourable moment of urging his request.

In short, then, " *exoriantur legati*," among us, who will shew to Europe at large, that the perfection of diplomatic wisdom and skill does not consist in a scrupulous adherence to antiquated usages and formalities, and to principles borrowed from less enlightened times; but in a general knowledge of the world and the ways of men, in a behaviour equally calculated to soften national pride and prejudices, and to win confidence and esteem, and in that energy, decision, and firmness, which can alone lay the foundation of successful conduct, in public as well as private affairs.

ESSAY X.

ON THE DUTIES OF ATTORNIES.

IF the importance of a man in the scale of civil society be weighed according to his power of injuring or benefiting his fellow-citizens, and such a mode of estimate is pretty generally formed, it will then appear, that those who follow the profession of an Attorney or solicitor in our courts of law and equity, may reasonably arrogate to themselves no small pretensions to public notice. To demonstrate the justness of this observation, we shall proceed to deduce the origin and nature of the legal functions of an Attorney; and then presume to suggest a line of conduct for his adoption, which would not impoverish his usual stock of gains, and yet entitle him to the respect and gratitude of his country.

An Attorney at law, so called from *attornatus*, which word implies, to be put in the turn of another, corresponds to the procurator or proctor of the civilians or canonists. In periods when each man took upon himself to avenge his private wrongs, summary justice could be easily exercised: every suitor was then (according to the old Gothic constitution) obliged to appear in person to prosecute or defend his suit, unless the king's letters patent authorised his absence: but as soon as the litigious spirit of men increased, and we may suppose that very soon to have happened, it was found expedient to permit Attornies to prosecute and defend any action in the absence of the parties to the suit*.

To modern times however we must look for the exertions of that corps being called forth by suitable encouragements; for our ancestors had such frequent recourse to the simple dictates of nature and reason, in the adjustment of their disputes, that an act of Parliament passed in the 33d year of the reign of Henry III. expressly states, that before that period there had not been more than six or eight Attornies in Norfolk or Suffolk; in which time, it remarks, *great tranquility* reigned†; but the number had increased to twenty-

* This convenient mode of proceeding was first recognised in Statute Westminster, II. cap. x. agreeably to that in the Roman law : cum olim in usu fuisset, alterius nomine agi non posse, sed quia hoc non minimam incommoditatem habebat, cœperunt homines per procuratores litigare.

† Quo tempore magna tranquillitas regnabat.—*See Blackstone's Com-*

four, to the great prejudice and inconvenience of both counties. It therefore enacted, that there should be only six Attornies in Norfolk, six in Suffolk, and two in the city of Norwich.

It is a truth as rare as it is glorious, that England is perhaps the only country upon the face of the earth, in which justice, civil and criminal, is administered with purity ; and happy should we be to add, that cheapness and dispatch were likewise the inseparable concomitants of our judicature; but the fact is not to be denied, however it may be lamented, that the volumes of our law books are swollen to such an enormous extent, that few purses can procure them ; and are so contradictory one to another in their sense, that still fewer capacities can digest them. When one volume therefore brings us out of a labyrinth, the next perhaps plunges us into another, more difficult to unravel than the famous Cretan maze. In short, such is the multiplicity and intricacy of the statutes, the variety of reports, the nicety of conveyancing, the dexterity of pleading, and the confusion, uncertainty, and expence, which these occasion, that after the defendant in a cause has

mentaries, vol. III. p. 25. The learned editor, Mr. Christian, adds, that as it does not appear this statute was ever repealed, it might be curious to enquire how it was originally evaded.---Note 11.

obtained a verdict in his favor, he is probably beggared by his success*. The well-known line of Dr. Young may be quoted, and, alas! be reckoned no paradox:—

" He is redressed, till he is undone."

If then the sons of sophistry and chicanery be so successful in their arts, as to make fraud sometimes assume before juries+ the garb of honesty, and so totally devoid of integrity, as seldom to reconcile the common law to common sense, but when it promotes their own private advantage; we must attribute no small share of an evil pregnant with such afflicting and mischievous consequences, to the conduct of Attornies or solicitors ‡. All general observations are doubtless liable to excep-

* ————; ex quo illud, summum jus summa injuria, factum est jam tritum sermone proverbium.—*Cicero, De Officiis, lib. i. cap. xi.*

+ The unanimity required by a verdict, in this country, in order to make it legal, may perhaps, in the case of an advocate blinding the judgment of an obstinate and tenacious juryman, be productive of much real injustice. We are not ignorant, that sages of the law affirm, this unanimity gives great credit and weight to a verdict; but our wise ancestors, it will be remembered, in the reigns of Henry I. Henry II. and Edward I. thought otherwise; for then, if the jurors dissented, sometimes there was added a number equal to the greater party, & they were to give up their verdict by twelve of the old jurors and the jurors so added.

‡ These names are indiscriminately used by most writers; yet, legally speaking, he only can be called a Soliciter who is admitted to practise in the Court of Chancery.

tions: nevertheless the fact is notorious, that although the majority perhaps of those who make our laws their study, illustrate and confirm in their daily practice the established maxim, that *actus legi, nulli facit injuriam,* yet the most plenary evidence can be produced, of numbers in the profession realizing the picture just now drawn.

In proportion then to the mischiefs arising from the scandalous abuses exemplified by this description of persons, ought to be our indignation against those who do all in their power to form and bring them to maturity. Without acquiescing in the pernicious saying, that where much is alledged, something must be true, we can however admit the veracity of the assertion, that many Attornies are not only a disgrace to their profession, but a dishonor to mankind. Nor do we conceive it very uncharitable in us to suspect, that few of them, on the eve of being inrolled, are mindful of that statute in the fourth year of Henry IV. which enjoins, that none are to be admitted into their order, but such as are virtuous, learned, and sworn to their duty. In extenuation of overlooking that statute in their conduct, and substituting low artifice and obsequious insincerity in the place of disinterested honesty, it is but just to add, that the whole of the fault does not center with them, but some part of it must be given to that class of clients whose riches are equal to their litigiousness, and whose want of honor is superior to both. Men such as these, who think they can do conscientiously whatever they can do legally, (and the race, it is to be regretted, is very prolific,) always wish to make, and often succeed in making, their Attornies disregard every consideration of humanity and probity which may obstruct the gaining of their cause ; and always are accustomed to measure out their reward to them, according to the degree of villainy they have displayed for gaining their ends.

While wealth is in the habit of being converted to such purposes, are we to expect that the grievances which the public have so long and so justly complained of, will soon cease? Can it excite wonder, if the baits thrown out by those opulent wretches '(for, with them, *" quid salvis infamia nummis")* to a young man who has a fortune to seek, and a family to maintain, have not a powerful effect in determining the character of his principles? He must be little read in the volume of human nature who cannot discover, that after some ineffectual appeals to the tribunal of his conscience*, the temp-

* Let me not, however, be understood as representing a person so unhappily circumstanced, being without a single sentiment of remorse, at

tation to become an instrument of fraud and violence is too great for him to withstand: let us not then, in expressing our detestation of the effects of their proceedings, forget also to arraign the causes of them.

It is an observation, the truth of which has been so generally admitted as even to have passed into a proverb, that only a knave is fit to be employed in the concerns of the law. What a seeming inconsistency is here asserted, and how humbling to the dignity of the human character, that an honest man should be esteemed the most improper character to be employed in a profession, with which the existence and support of society are so inseparably connected.

To rescue the character of Attornies from this degrading imputation, and to enable them more often to apply to their conduct the honourable words of *Rightly*, in the *Heiress*, "When I detect wrong, and vindicate the sufferer, I feel the spirit of the law of England

once completely and systematically lost to every honourable feeling. There must be stages of wickedness in the very worst of men. Even he, who had attained the highest pitch of hardened reprobacy and atrocity that is any where exhibited in the records of authentic history, was at one period of his life just and merciful :—it is related of the sanguinary Nero, that in the early part of his reign, being requested to put his signet for the execution of a malefactor, he burst into the humane exclamation, " Quam vellem me nescire litteras :"--I wish I had never learnt to read.—*See Suetonius in Nerone, lib. vi. cap. x.*

and the pride of a practitioner," we shall venture to think, that the practice of the following rules would go no inconsiderable way to secure that most important and desirable end.

The law in its origin was doubtless designed to distribute right to every one, and this is strongly expressed in the Greek word νομος*. The uniform observance, therefore, of the principles of honesty in their dealings, we would, in the first place, endeavour to impress upon the minds of Attornies; for though particular points of interest may sometimes be accomplished by indirect cunning, it must be generally admitted, that he who deviates from the path of honesty, will seldom find this deviation rewarded by superior good fortune. To execute his business with reputation, an Attorney ought never to lose sight of those plain, simple, and irrefragable principles of justice, on which all law is, or ought to be founded; he should, therefore, employ his utmost means to discourage suits for trivial or vexatious demands; he should manifest himself so great a lover of truth, as to set his face decidedly against the production of those sort of witnesses, who are disposed to think that a lie is pardonable, if it be serviceable; he should feel

* Απο τυ νεμειν—a distribuendo.

an abhorrence of brow-beating and intimidating the
adverse party, or of taking an advantage of an over-
sight in his counsel or Attorney, or of want of form
in the pleadings, unless when he is on the defensive
side, and his client's cause is the cause of injured
justice; he should not pride himself on his dexterity
in the infamous arts of misleading the court, pro-
longing the cause, or enhancing the costs, though at
the expence of the opponent; and he deserves to be
pointed out to the scorn and execration of every honest
man, if he encourages an appeal from court to court,
without having the strongest conviction on his mind,
that the decision was completely unsatisfactory in the
point of substantial justice. To be true also to his
own fame, and to the sacred rules of justice, if, while
the suit is pending, he should discover that his client's
claim or defence is ill-grounded, he ought not to shrink
from delivering it as his decisive opinion, that the suit
should be dropped against his adversary; and with the
same explicit plainness he should add, if such adversary
be poor or aggrieved by having his just right withheld
from him, that ample remuneration is strictly his due.
It might likewise be fairly said, that he was hostile to
every principle of humanity who did not advise his
client to be merciful, when the law had securely fixed
him on the *vantage ground.*

In all criminal prosecutions an Attorney ought ever to keep in mind, that though it is a primary part of his duty to be prompt and resolute against hardened and daring offenders, he is not less bound to abstain from employing all reprehensible expedients for their condemnation. In giving advice on mortgages, or in any pecuniary concerns, he would deservedly have much odium to bear, who is not earnest from motives of compassion alone, abstracted from all legal considerations, in discountenancing usury, and every improper advantage taken of the necessitous. When the debtor is insolvent, it is the obvious duty of the Attorney to promote equality in the distribution of his effects among those who are entitled to them: and when it is clear that a man has fallen into poverty by an unavoidable series of misfortunes, that circumstance ought to operate upon the Attorney, and call him to step forward voluntarily, in mitigating any excess of persecution and hostility on the part of his creditors.

An Attorney who cannot preserve a profound secrecy in settlements, and in family transactions, may be considered as guilty not only of one of those improprieties which are the objects of simple disapprobation, but of one of those acts which entitle him to meet the severest reprehension from the afflicting, and oftentimes fatal consequences, which such a violation of trust occasions.

That many wives, daughters, and sons, have well-grounded reasons to deplore, deeply to deplore, the commanding influence possessed by Attornies over their husbands and parents in the disposition of their estates by will, is an assertion unfortunately too true, we fear, to be controverted. According then to the amiableness or wickedness of the character of the Attorney, will be the great and irreparable good or evil done by him: if he be actuated by virtuous intentions, instead of dwelling upon any hasty sally of resentment dropped by a wife or child against a husband or parent in an unguarded moment, and thereby administering fuel to a flame which would otherwise have died away of itself, he will omit the mention of no circumstance which is likely to restore peace and happiness between them; in short, it will excite in his heart sentiments of the most deep and sincere disappointment and anguish to see any one disinherited, or deprived of his just portion, through passion, caprice, or an unforgiving temper. When extreme old age, or long sickness, can give birth even to the most distant suspicion of the testator's intellects being affected, an upright Attorney will take especial care to procure witnesses of the most spotless reputation; and under these circumstances, if he does not discourage all artful requests which may be made to such a person to bequeath his wealth to charitable uses, his conduct will not be less offensive to the opinions of honest and reflecting men, than prejudicial to the interests of the surviving relations.

If an Attorney would thus discharge his duty, his profession would then command that respect which it really deserves; and the justice of the complaint be no longer recognized, at least be confined to a few, that the prosperity of Attornies is a libel upon the nation.

We are not to be told, that for an Attorney to act in the manner we have pointed out, he has to encounter the low interests, the passions, the prejudices, and oftentimes the unjust reproaches of mankind. In addition to these trials, no very easy ones to surmount, another will present itself, in which it is still more difficult to attain success; namely, that of acquiring such a complete dominion over his own passions, as to be inaccessible to every present and apparent interest, that may in the least endanger the establishment of his fame as an upright man: but in thus endeavouring to stand forward in the cause of reason and justice, and to exert his utmost to serve his fellow-creatures, should he after all be disappointed of his reward from the good and virtuous, he will nevertheless secure what is, however, of still more importance, the approbation of his own conscience, and that of the Supreme Legislator and Judge of the Universe.

ESSAY XI.

ON THE CONDUCT AND CHARACTER OF CHRISTINA, QUEEN
OF SWEDEN.

THERE are few sovereigns in modern Europe who
have been the subject of more applause and censure
than Christina, Queen of Sweden. The voluntary
abdication of her throne has been viewed by some in
no other light than as an infamous desertion of her
public duties, for the indulgence of ease and for the
enjoyment of private pleasure; although others have
professed to discern in that act, the rare and laudable
moderation of the true philosopher. Her conversion
to the Romish church filled one-half of Europe with
grief, shame, and indignation, and has induced the
Protestants too hastily to assert, that her mind, in
the choice of her religion, was only influenced by a
sense of interest ; while, from that circumstance alone,
the Catholics saw a thousand excellencies in her character, in which they would otherwise have found, perhaps, nothing but what was calculated to create alarm
or to excite disgust. Her real learning has not been

more suspected than her real chastity, although the most unbounded panegyrics have been heaped upon both: in short, every great and good quality has been bestowed upon Christina by the zeal of her adherents, and every bad one by the malice of her enemies.

But though the immoderate approbation or immoderate aversion of several writers has led them into unjustifiable extremes, in speaking of Christina, yet it must be confessed, that the character of the daughter of Gustavus is too unimportant to merit the two ponderous quartos of her historian Arckenholtz[*]. It is not our design then to fill whole pages with a tedious enumeration, as he has done, of every trifling event in her varied life; yet with such a guide, and with the copious materials which he has provided, we may be enabled, in the shape of an historical essay, to lay before our readers those parts of her public and private life which are most deserving of their notice.

Christina was scarcely six years old, when a cannon ball, at Lutzen, put an end to the victorious career of her renowned father, Gustavus Adolphus, who had carried the desolation of war from the centre of Bohemia to the mouth of the Scheldt, from the banks of the Po to

[*] See Memoi es sur Christine, Reine de Suede, a Amsterdam, 1751.

the coasts of the Baltic, and had displayed to the oppressor of Germany, the Emperor Ferdinand, the tremendous uncertainty of human greatness. In the plan which the celebrated Oxenstiern, the friend and minister of that great hero, drew out for the regency, we may discern a regard for the rights of the nobility and for the liberties of the people, which reflects honour upon his memory, as it shews his dislike to that form of government which invests an individual with an unlimited authority.

At a very early age Christina is represented to have evinced a remarkable thirst for knowledge. We are solicited to believe, that in her infancy she had made such great proficiency in the Greek tongue, as to be capable of reading Thucidydes and Polybius, and of comparing the different merits of those historians. By the particular wish of the estates of Sweden, a great portion of her time was also devoted to the study of the Bible, as that book, they justly observe in an express memoir, is the source of all other histories. It will not be expected or desired that we should enter into any detail of the minority of Christina, nor upon the reciprocal and perhaps equally just complaints between her and her allies, when she had taken the reins of government into her own hands, as the relation of those circumstances would extend this essay beyond its proper limits.

One of the first acts of Christina's reign, which we esteem worthy of remembrance, was her confirming the title which Grotius had received from the Chancellor Oxenstiern, of Ambassador to France. By the fury of political and religious factions, that illustrious scholar had been driven from his country, and obliged to seek an asylum in France: upon his coming there Cardinal Richelieu had given him a pension, but soon withdrew it, because he did not flatter his literary talents*. Grotius had, however, attracted the notice of Gustavus Adolphus, and after his quitting France he was received at his court with every mark of respect suitable to his distinguished merit. In ratifying then the appointment of her chancellor, Christina had the satisfaction of rewarding a man of real genius and virtue, in a manner correspondent with her greatness; of mortifying the Hollanders, whom she disliked; and of deeply wounding the pride of the Cardinal, by enabling the object of his aversion to treat him with all the independence of an equal.

* The chief cause of the Cardinal's displeasure against Grotius arose from his having omitted to praise him in the dedication of his immortal Treatise, *De Jure Belli et Pacis*, which he inscribed to Louis XIII. of France.

[1647.] Devoted to letters, and possessed not of the warlike spirit of her father, it is easy to conceive that the Queen of Sweden should feel extremely anxious for the conclusion of the peace of Westphalia: the obstacles which retarded that event arose more, however, from the animosity and jealousy of the different ministers, than even from the infinite variety of interests which they had to adjust. Count Oxenstiern, son of the great chancellor, and Alder Salvius, chancellor of the court, were the plenipotentiaries of Sweden; and greater division did not exist between them, than among those of France and Germany. The first was by no means disposed to exert his abilities for the effecting a general peace, because he considered the continuation of the war as no less favourable to the glory of Sweden, than prejudicial to the selfish views of France: on the other hand, Salvius, the favourite of the Queen, warmly entered into all her wishes upon that subject, and therefore endeavoured, as far as lay in his power, to frustrate the designs of his colleague. We are told of a discourse that Christina made to the senate when she appointed Salvius a member of that august assembly, although he was of mean extraction, which ought to be engraved in the hearts of all kings: " When it is a question of good advice and safe counsels," said she, " we do not demand sixteen descents, but what is to be done. The abilities of Salvius would doubtless still be conspicuous, if he could deduce his origin from persons of family: he must then esteem it an honour that no other reproach can be made against him but the want of high birth. The assistance, however, of able men is required by us; if then the sons of rank possess talents, they will make their fortunes as well as those whose strong claims of merit must likewise supersede the ideal prerogatives of family."

[A. D. 1648.] The peace of Westphalia was at last accomplished, to the reciprocal satisfaction of the greater part of the interested powers. No one, however, was so violent in his expressions of anger against the promoters of it as Innocent X. for by that event all his ambitious views which he had formed, as sovereign Pontiff, of humbling the pride of the Protestants, were thwarted. As a public proof of his displeasure against the active part which Christina had taken in that important affair, he published a bull, in which he refused her the title of the Queen of Sweden, and caused his nuncio at Vienna to post it upon the gates of that city, but the Emperor ordered it to be torn down. Innocent prudently offered no second attack with his spiritual weapons against Christina.

Several advantageous proposals of marriage were now made to Christina, but her love of freedom prevailed over any temporary inclination she might have felt for that state. The King of Spain, Philip IV. was one of those who sought her hand, but he soon dropped his pretensions, on the consideration, that if his suit were successful, it would oblige him to abstain from treating the Protestants as heretics. The courtship paid to her by her cousin, Charles Gustavus, the Prince Palatin, was the most agreeable to the Swedish nation; but whatever was the motive, she soon came to the resolution of declining his proposals. In order, moreover, that a stop might be put to the importunate addresses which she received from her people, to fix her choice of a husband, she prevailed on the estates of Sweden to declare Charles Gustavus her successor: by this step she at once freed herself from any further troublesome applications on the part of her people to change her condition, ensured tranquillity to Sweden, and prevented all disputes with regard to the succession.

[A. D. 1650.] The excessive attachment shewn by Christina to men of genius and learning, urged her to seek the correspondence and society of the celebrated Descartes, who was put in the expurgatory index at Rome, for having believed the astronomical observations on the movement of the earth, rather than the bulls of the Popes; and who was persecuted in Holland, for having substituted the true method of philosophizing in the room of the jargon of the schools. The precursor of Newton hesitated a long time whether he should accept her invitation, as he put his liberty at so high a price, that, according to his usual expression, all the kings of the world could not purchase it. The difference of climates, also, was another principal reason which deterred him from undertaking a voyage to Stockholm. In his letter upon this occasion to M. Chanut, the French ambassador in Sweden, and a most intimate friend, he observes, that a man born in the gardens of Touraine, and retired in a land where he had less of honey indeed, but perhaps more of milk, than in the promised land of the Israelites, could not easily resolve to quit it, in order to live in a country of bears, among rocks and ice.

After some further delays and excuses, the philosopher, however, thought proper to repair to the Swedish court: his reception there was such as must have gratified his utmost pride. The Queen exempted him from all the subjection and restraint which are imposed upon courtiers, as she presently found they were not suited to his temper or character. At five in the morning she commenced her studies with him, for the first part of the day was invariably devoted to the improvement of her understanding. As the chief of a sect, Descartes expected all his opinions and his tastes to be adopted by his disciples: it did not there-fore meet his approbation, that Christina should turn occasionally from philosophy to the study of languages: he could not, also, conceal his dislike at her being sur-rounded with such a crowd of pedants, as led strangers to say, that Sweden would soon be governed by gram-marians. So freely did he remonstrate with her on these two points, that he drew upon himself the resentment of Vossius, the instructor of the Queen in the Greek tongue, of whom our Charles the Second said, in derision of his incredulity and superstition, that he believed every thing except the Bible. Chris-tina did not, however, so far comply with the ap-plication of Descartes as to abandon her Greek books, although she gave him such an obliging answer upon this subject, that he still retained hopes of her sub-mitting in the end to his wishes. In the mean time she expressed such uncommon sentiments of regard for him, and heaped so many marks of her favour upon him, that, according to the scandalous reports of the times, the grammarians of Stockholm accelerated his death by poison: but science, we must believe, has too close a connexion with virtue, for the commission of atrocious crimes to be often found in the lives of scholars,

Christina now began to find that, as Queen of Sweden, more important tasks were allotted to her than those of studying the learned languages, and paying attention to learned foreigners. The embarrassed state of the public finances, occasioned by her indiscriminate liberality, paved the way for general discontent; and her imperious conduct in her family and court, together with her amorous propensities, rendered her both odious and disgusting in the eyes of good and reflecting men.

[1651.] These unpleasant circumstances seemed to have hastened her design of resigning the sceptre into the hands of her kinsman, Charles Gustavus, for we find that in this year she made a public communication of this intention to the senate. The united solicitations of her appointed successor and of her subjects, who still contemplated the daughter of the great Gustavus, in spite of all her imprudencies and excesses, with sentiments of affection and reverence, obliged her, however, to continue for some time longer the exercise of the royal authority.

Some writers pretend, that in the following year, 1652, Christina began to give the most unequivocal proofs of her intention to abandon the faith of her ancestors: but the moment of grace was certainly not yet arrived; for in answer to an highly complimentary letter which M. Godeau, Bishop of Venice, addressed to her that year, after saying to him, that the good folks of France were so accustomed to flatter, that she did not dare complain of so general a custom, and therefore she was not surprized at receiving his praises, although she is thankful for them, she proceeds to express a wish, that his mind possessed the same light as her's did upon matters of religion*. Now this is surely a very unsuitable declaration to fall from one upon the eve of becoming a Catholic: and in a letter which she wrote in the same year to Prince Frederic of Hesse, to dissuade him from embracing the Roman religion, we may discern the same decided inclination to the Protestant communion.

The strong attachment which Christina really felt to the cause of letters, and the undistinguishing pa-

---

* Il y à long tems que je suis persuadée que les choses que je crois sont celles que l'on doit croire. Ce seroit plutôt à moi a souhaiter que parmi tant de belles lumieres dont votre ami est eclairé, vous eussiez encore celles que j'ai sur cette matiere.—*See Memoires sur Christine, tom. I. p. 215.*

tronage which she gave to its professors, very naturally excited the highest applauses from the literati of Sweden and of other countries; but in the two hundred panegyrics which **M.** Arckenholtz reckons to have been bestowed upon Christina, we may in vain look for her real character. In her intercourse with men of learning she departed so widely from the dignity of the Queen, and became so much of the pedant in petticoats, that her intellectual attainments, so far from producing her any real glory, may be said, in a great measure, to have diminished the lustre of her character as a sovereign: the levity too, or rather licentiousness of behaviour, in which she so often indulged before them, must have even secretly inspired the disgust of those men, who were led equally by inclination and interest to conceal her vices, and to proclaim her real or pretended virtues. Of this disposition to speak and to act in the company of men of learning, in a manner inconsistent with the modesty of a female, innumerable instances remain; but the following will be quite sufficient to confirm this assertion:—Salmasius, so renowned for his critical skill, and extensive and profound knowledge of languages, whom Milton pleased himself with the malignant idea of having killed in their last dispute,

was one of the first scholars who had visited the court
of Christina, and possessed, in a remarkable degree,
the esteem and confidence of his royal pupil. It
happened once that she paid him a visit during a fit
of illness, and found him in bed reading a book,
which, upon her entrance, he immediately closed.
" Ha, ha," said the Queen, " let us see what engages
your attention: come, shew us some good passages."
Salmasius having pointed out one of the best, she cast
her eye over it, and afterwards said to her favourite
Sparre, better known by the name of La belle Com-
tesse, who accompanied her on this occasion, " Come
hither, Sparre, and look at this fine book of devotion,
entitled, *Le Moyen de parvenir*: come, now, read us
this page: but Sparre had not proceeded three
lines before the indecency of the language obliged
her to stop: her blushes, however, and confusion,
only served to heighten the Queen's pleasure, and
almost convulsed with laughter, she insisted upon her
finishing the page, in spite of every remonstrance she
made against the uncommonly offensive expressions
in it*.

The moment was at length arrived when the fatigues
and cares of sovereignty became so insupportable to

* See this anecdote in *Menagiana*, *tom. IV. p.* 323.

Christina, that no persuasions could induce her to bear them any longer. The many hours she was obliged to allot to the discharge of the various duties of her high station, had so completely oppressed her spirits and preyed upon her health, that when the secretaries brought her dispatches to sign, she fancied, to borrow one of her own curious expressions, she *saw the devil.* In the following letter which she addressed to M. Chanut, upon her resolution of abdicating the crown, there is an affectation of superior sagacity, and an ostentatious approbation of her own conduct, by no means compatible with the modesty of conscious merit :—" In retiring from the stage," said she, " I give myself no uneasiness about the plaudits; I know that the scene which I have represented is not according to the common laws of the theatre, but a masculine and vigorous design rarely pleases all descriptions of persons; I permit, however, every one to judge according to his genius: I cannot indeed take away this liberty, and would not if it were in my power." In another part of the letter she seems inclined to treat with a supercilious contempt all those who should presume to shew their displeasure at the step she was about to take; while the truth of this remark has certainly been much and justly disputed by an unbiassed posterity:—" I have preferred the conservation of the state before all other considerations, and have sacrificed every thing with joy to its interests; and I have nothing to reproach myself with in that administration, which I possessed without pride, and abandoned with facility."

Before, however, Christina had resigned the sceptre into the hands of Charles Gustavus, an act which has been so variously accounted for by the ingenious conjectures of contemporary historians, but which, after all, may be most safely and reasonably ascribed to the desire of freedom, and to an aversion from the toils of government; she made an attempt to place her successor in such a precarious and dependant situation, that, had he not firmly resisted it, he could only have been considered as her representative. She wished to be fixed in a state of absolute independence; to have the liberty of remaining in any part of Sweden she pleased; to see no change in the appointments which she had made; and to reserve for herself the greater part of the kingdom. This last condition seems to have originated from the advice which Whitelocke, the ambassador of Cromwell, gave, when she intimated to him her design of abdicating the crown ;—" to be warned by the conduct of Philip to his father, Charles V.

after his abdication; and therefore to reserve that country in her possession, out of which her reserved revenue should be issued;—for, when money is to be paid out of a prince's treasury," adds the ambassador, " it is not always ready and certain*." When Christina found that Charles would not condescend to become a mere titular king, she had the art of turning her propositions into a compliment to him, by saying, that " she made them with no other view but to discover his real character; and that she was now perfectly satisfied, that Charles Gustavus was worthy to reign, since he so well understood the rights of a monarch."

A few days before her departure from Sweden, Christina caused a medal to be struck, the legend of which must have excited a smile of contempt from her ambitious successor,—" That Parnassus was better than a throne." When she had reached a small stream on the frontiers of Sweden, which separated Denmark

---

* If Whitelocke does not deliver his sentiments with the dignity of an ambassador, it must be at least acknowledged that he speaks with the freedom of a man, especially in that part of the conversation where he tells her, that " the same persons who now fawn upon her, she must expect to find, when she is no longer Queen, disposed to put affronts and scorn upon her."—*See his Journal on the Swedish Embassy, vol. I. p. 366.*

from that kingdom, she waved her hand and exclaimed, "At last I behold myself at liberty and out of Sweden, whither I hope never to return."

As the constitution of Christina was inured to fatigue by hunting and other strong exercises, she performed the greater part of the journey through Denmark and Germany on horseback, clad in male attire. To whatever town she came, the people flocked in multitudes, to see the woman, who passed in the judgment of many for the most shining constellation of her age. The singularity of her dress attracted as much notice as the freedom of her manners: she usually appeared in the waistcoat, hat, and collar, of a man, with a black ribbon carelessly tied round her neck, and with a short petticoat which descended no lower than to the middle of her leg. We are likewise informed, (for these trifles have been detailed with a minute importance by many writers,) that she *bowed* upon introductions, and paid her compliments after the style of a man. The enemies of Christina have not confined their misrepresentations to the qualities of her mind, but have extended them to her person. If we listen to them, we must believe that her figure was deformed, her complexion sallow, her eyes dim-sighted, her nose of a most preposterous

length*, and the colour of her teeth the very opposite
to pearly whiteness: but in the fair and impartial nar-
rative of Whitelocke, we learn, that if she did not
possess all the beauty of her sex, her countenance was
animated and interesting; " and though her person
was of the smaller size, her mien and carriage were
very noble+."

[1655.] Already had Christina prepared for the
change of her religion, by visiting all the monasteries
and churches which she found in her route: at length,
after having embraced the Roman Catholic faith at
Brussels, she publicly abjured Lutheranism in the
cathedral church at Inspruck‡, and took this device,
which left a doubt in the minds of many, if she was
not virtually as much a pagan as a papist—*Fata viam
invenient.*

The proselytism of Christina, like her abdication,
was equally the theme of panegyric and invective.
The highest praises were of course bestowed on this act
by the Catholics; while the Protestants pretended, that

---

* Son nez est plus long que son pied.---*See this hyperbolical expression
in La Vie de Christine, Rèyne de Suede, à Stockholm,* 1667, *p.* 39.

+ See Journal of the Swedish Embassy, vol. I. p. 235.

‡ For a detailed account of the ceremonies attending her conversion,
see *History of the Queen of Swedland, p.* 150, 166.

she was indifferent to all religions, and that convenience was the only motive which influenced her to embrace Popery; since, by professing its tenets, she was more fully enabled to gratify the wish she had, to spend the remainder of her life in Italy, the favoured abode of the arts and sciences. In proof of this indifference, they relate, that in Sweden it was her usual custom during the performance of divine service, if the discourse of the minister did not please her, to play with two favourite spaniels, which generally attended upon such occasions, or to chat with some of her attendants; or else to express her impatience by making such a noice with her fan, as could not have been otherwise interpreted by the priest, than into a mandate for his immediate silence*. They likewise affirm, that whenever any allusion was made to the stupendous miracles wrought by Moses, it was her constant saying, that she would undertake to demonstrate the falsehood of the pretended miraculous passage of the Israelites through the Red Sea, by the victory which Numenius, one of the generals of Antiochus, had obtained over the Persians, at the same season, place, and manner, as Moses did over Pharoah, by observing the flux and reflux of that sea†: while, to shew also that she was no

* See La Vie de Christine, Rèyne de Suede, p. 75.
† Page 16, 20.

more a Catholic than a Lutheran, they instanced the reply which she made to the Jesuits of Louvain, when they promised her a place near St. Bridget of Sweden: *" It would afford me more pleasure to obtain a seat among the sages."*

But though we entertain some suspicions that she never broke out into so daring a tone of infidelity, as to dispute the divine authority of the Bible, yet her excessive admiration of the writings of Plato and of other Greek philosophers may be supposed to have abated much of the religion, zeal, and devotion which are said to have marked her early years. It is also certain, that during her stay at Rome she paid more visits to the works of the great masters in that city, than to Alexander VII. who then filled the papal chair, or to any of the sacred orators. Of all the fine arts, she seems to have possessed a more thorough knowledge of sculpture than of any other, and to have been most delighted with it. It happened one day, while she was admiring a marble statue of the celebrated chevalier Bernini, which represented Truth, that a cardinal who stood near her, took occasion to observe, that she loved truth more than did other princes; *" But all truths,"* answered she, *" are not of marble."*

[1656.] An epidemical disorder which appeared at

this time at Rome gave Christina a fair pretence of gratifying her love of-novelty by taking a journey to France. Being apprised of her intention, the king of France directed that his illustrious visitor should be received with great splendor in every city through which she passed. Accordingly all ranks of people vied with each other in offering her tokens of their respect and homage. - Upon her arrival at Fontainbleau, she was treated with every distinction due to her royal birth, character, and accomplishments; and being astonished at the ceremonial of the court, she demanded upon what account the ladies testified such eagerness to kiss her: "*Is it*," said she, "*because I resemble a man?*"

During the abode of Christina in France, the men there found, or affected to find, such a combination of endowments in her character as were never before united in the same person: but we are instructed to believe, that she was no favorite with her own sex. The ladies of France did not at all relish her keen and pointed remarks in answer to their obsequious flatteries ; nor her blunt interrogatories respecting their criminal amours. Her swearing, a vice to which she was much addicted, gave, it must be confessed, just cause of offence to many, while her superior understanding excited the envy of all. Those who pretended best to appreciate her merits, compared her to the castle of Fontainbleau,—grand, but irregular. Madame de Motteville, who seems, from what reason we are ignorant, to have been animated with a particular ill-will towards her, relates, as a proof we suppose of her depraved taste and passions, that Ninon, the celebrated courtezan, was the only female in France for whom she shewed any marks of esteem, or visited with any real pleasure.

From Fontainbleau, Christina proceeded to Paris. Having surveyed the city, and received a ceremonial visit from the magistrates, she was presented by the famous Menage to the French Academy; and as it was esteemed by the literati a sort of title to celebrity to be introduced to a Queen, who had descended from her throne in the prime of life for the sake of philosophizing, and who sought the acquaintance of every man of literary reputation with the utmost avidity, Menage, who served as a master of ceremonies to her during the time she remained in Paris, received so many applications to confer that honor, that, for fear of offending some, he withheld it from none. This occasioned Christina to say, that M. Menage was acquainted with a great many persons of merit.

[1657.] Fond of balls, ballets, and all the amusements of youth, and likewise delighted with the company and conversation of men of learning, Christina, as she could enjoy all those pleasures in perfection at Paris, felt such regret at quitting it, that she had scarcely revisited Italy, before she returned to France. This second journey to that kingdom was undertaken, as was alledged, for political purposes; but it was only remarkable for the commission of a deed which has deservedly entitled the memory of Christina to the execration of posterity—the murder of Monaldeschi, her chief equerry. Every circumstance attending the death of this unfortunate nobleman, so strongly marks the vindictive spirit of the Queen, as cannot but excite the utmost horror and disgust in the mind of the humane reader.

On the tenth of November this bloody scene was performed, in the gallery of Les Cerfs, in the palace of Fontainbleau*. Father Le Bel, an eye witness and relater of it, informs us, that upon that day he was conducted by a domestic of the Queen's into the above-mentioned gallery, where he found her, the Marquis, and three other persons, two of whom observed a respectful distance. When the Queen had finished her

* The reader will find Father Le Bel's circumstantial account of this affair, in La Vie de Rèyne de Suede, p. 134, 154.

reproaches against the Marquis for having betrayed her confidence, which she made him confess he had done, by shewing him his own signature to certain papers, an awful pause ensued, and the assassins drew their swords; at the sight of which the unhappy victim, in the agony of despair, pursued the Queen to the different parts of the gallery, supplicating for pardon. She listened to him all the time with the utmost coolness, and at last quitted the apartment, having addressed these emphatic words to the priests :—*"Fathers, I leave you this man; prepare him for his death, and take care of his soul."* Before, however, the atrocious crime was perpetrated, the chief of the assassins was so deeply moved by the urgent entreaties of the Marquis, that he went in person to the Queen, to try if he could obtain his pardon. Father Le Bel also made the same request, and ventured to hint to her, that she would more consult her reputation, by either forgiving the Marquis, or delivering him into the hands of public justice. She was too much bent upon the wreaking of her vengeance to turn a willing ear to any petition or remonstrance which they could offer. When the last moments of the Marquis were over, for the inhumanity of his executioners suffered him to lie some time in the agonies of death, Father Le Bel waited on the Queen in an adjoining room, where she had remained during the whole of the transaction; and from him we also learn, that such was the amazing ferocity of her temper, that she dismissed him without manifesting any one sign of remorse for the detestable act she had caused to be done; unless indeed our readers will consider as one, the presenting him with a hundred livres, *to say mass for the soul of the Marquis.*

This deed, which renders the name of Christina infamous in the judgment of posterity, was then, incredible to relate, viewed with such indulgence, that sage lawyers and grave historians even proposed it, as a serious question, Whether or not a Queen, who has quitted the throne, has a right to take away the life of her domestics without any legal trial? Among the supporters of this question, which could only have originated from the basest flattery to Christina, we are both astonished and concerned to find the illustrious name of Leibnitz, the man who, in the character of teacher of jurisprudence, aspired to reform the laws of nature and of nations! For, if we examine into the offence of Monaldeschi, it will surely not be maintained by any writer, in whose breast exist those feelings of compassion which are natural to all men, that it was of a nature so heinous as could have been only expiated by assassination. Some writers we know have asserted, that the untimely end of Monaldeschi was occasioned by his having boasted publicly of Christina's passion for him; but others, with more truth and reason, have attributed it to the following circumstance:—That the Marquis, anxious to supplant Sentinelli, the chief favorite of Christina, had collected all the various scandalous tales which were spread abroad respecting them both; and having committed these to paper, in a feigned hand-writing, procured a servant to deliver this string of calumnies to the Queen—an insult which, in her mind, could only be atoned by his blood. Easily then may the assertion be accredited, that the remembrance of such barbarity served to plunge her occasionally into the deepest grief and melancholy.

But as cruelty inspires hatred and contempt, Christina thought proper to shorten her visit to France, in consequence of this affair: although the court might be said to manifest a seeming approbation of it by its silence; in the looks however of many, she read an undisguised abhorrence of her conduct. She therefore determined to pay a visit to England; but Cromwell, we are assured, had no sort of inclination to spend the money of his country in giving a splendid reception to a Queen who had resigned three crowns to

embrace a religion which he hated; and who, practised in the arts of dissimulation, might succeed in
discovering those secrets which it was his interest, as
well as his duty, to conceal from her knowledge.

After making some further stay in France, Christina
at last returned to Rome, where she had full leisure
to resign herself to her propensity, or rather passion,
for the arts and sciences, particularly chemistry, medals, and statues; while the Cardinal Azzoni, her
confidential friend, undertook the management of her
finances, which were much deranged from her excessive
profuseness, and the want of regularity in the payment
of the pension which Sweden had settled upon her.
Of a temper, however, too restless and intriguing to
remain in a state of profound tranquility for any length
of time, Christina soon embroiled herself in a dispute
with the Pope, Alexander VII. respecting the marriage
of her favourite Sentinelli and the Dutchess de Ceri.
To pacify that vain frivolous old man for the active
part she had taken in forwarding this match, in direct
opposition to his wishes, she occasionally appeared in
the public processions to receive his benediction; and
still further to gratify his pride of being thought the
author of her conversion, she retired to a convent,
that the world might think the love of religion would

lead her in time to become a nun; while the real motive of this temporary seclusion was, the opportunity it afforded her of escaping, in a great degree, from the troublesome visits of the Pontiff.

The sudden death of King Charles Gustavus, which happened in the commencement of the year 1660, determined Christina once more to revisit Sweden. Historians ascribe this resolution to a strong desire she felt at that time of remounting the throne: but her visit, whatever were the views and intentions she had of making it, was attended with the most mortifying and unhappy consequences to her, both as a Queen and a woman. The ancient subjects of Christina had ceased to remember their former love and respect for her, and now only contemplated her as a rash and inconsiderate woman, who had forsaken them to embrace a religion which they abhorred: the Estates of the kingdom, therefore, were not long before they issued orders for the pulling down of her chapel, and the dismissal of the Italian chaplains who had followed her: nor would they permit her to quit Sweden before she had made a second renunciation of her rights to the crown. All these circumstances obliged Christina to return again to Rome; and as, after this violent breach, every hope of retaining something more in Sweden than the appearance of majesty seemed now at an end, she was rash and indiscreet enough to say, she quitted with pleasure a country filled with so many knaves, tyrants, and heretics*.

The greater part of Italy was at this time thrown into the utmost consternation, by the Turks having attacked the island of Candia; and such were the strenuous, though ineffectual, efforts made by the Queen of Sweden to procure for Venice supplies of troops and money from the princes of Europe, that many were uncharitable enough to suspect that her laudable exertions in behalf of that republic, were to be placed only to the most interested motives.

Shortly afterwards the famous affair of the Corses happened, in which the King of France obliged the

---

* It is worthy of remark, that there are no words in our language which have been so much strained by abuse from their original innocent purport, to their present opprobrious signification, as these three words: *knaves*, *tyrants*, and *heretics*. The word *knave* is of Saxon derivation, and, in its original sense, meant any kind of serving man. In an old English translation of the Bible, called sometimes Archbishop Cranmer's edition of it, St. Paul is denominated the *knave* of Christ.——Every Latin scholar knows that the word *tyrant*, in its original signification, meant no more than a king, though it is now invariably used to denote an usurper or oppressor.——The word *heretic*, or *heresy*, is derived from the Greek verb αιρεω, which signifies to chuse. In the original sense of this term no odious idea was affixed to it, as we find that Josephus calls the sect of the Pharisees a heresy, though he himself was a Pharisee.

Pope to disband his guards, for having offered an insult to his ambassador at Rome; and not content with this humiliating atonement, compelled him to send his nephew to ask pardon, and also to erect a monument in his own capital, of the expulsion of the Corses, his guards. Christina was employed by Alexander as his intercessor in this serious affair; and he had soon reason to believe that her regret was not sincere at the ill success of her applications: his dislike therefore to her manifested itself upon so many occasions, that she took the resolution of once more returning to Sweden. Whilst she was sounding the Estates of the kingdom upon that measure, she passed her hours at Rome in the conversation and society of men of letters, and sometimes amused herself at their expence, by causing the most curious inscriptions to be put upon the legend of medals, which she had struck for this purpose*.

The conditions which the Senate placed upon the Queen's return to Sweden appeared so very hard, that

---

* She had the word MAKELOS put upon one legend; which enigma gave rise to many disputes among the learned men, and consequently afforded much entertainment to Christina. MAKELOS, in case our readers have any curiosity to know the meaning of it, is a pure Swedish word, which admits of a double sense, and signifies *incomparable*, and likewise *an unmarried person*.

she judged it proper to repair to Hamburgh, and to await there the opening of the approaching Diet, in order to be ready to avail herself of any circumstance which might contribute to render her negociations with it successful. Of all the orders of the state, the clergy, strange to relate, seemed more disposed than any other to advance her interests. The rest of the nation, disgusted with her dissimulation and intrigues, used the right which she had given to them, and refused almost all her demands. She then renounced Sweden for ever, and returned to Rome, where she passed the remainder of her days, despising, and perpetually at variance with, the Pope*; ill paid by her ancient subjects, forgotten by France, and but little esteemed by that nation which she had preferred to every other. Christina soon perceived, after her abdication, to quote the words of Nani, the historian of Venice, that " a queen without a kingdom was a divinity without a temple, of which the worship is quickly abandoned."

* Bishop Burnet relates, in the History of his own Times, vol. II. page 415, that Christina one day said to him, " It was certain the church was governed by the immediate care and providence of God, for none of the four Popes she had known since she came to Rome had common sense."

[1686.] In study* and devotion†, in acting by turns the character of a queen, converter‡, astrologer §, and in a correspondence with the learned and great of Europe, were the last years of Christina's life consumed. Of all her numerous epistolary productions, there is no letter which reflects more honor upon her memory, than that which she addressed to the Chevalier Terlon, the ambassador of France in Sweden, in consequence of Louis XIV. having revoked the edict of Nantz. In the following passages of this letter, so much sound sense and real humanity are discoverable, as cannot but

* It is conjectured by some, that at this time she began, and by others, finished, her Reflections sur la Vie et les Actions de grand Alexandre. It would have been better perhaps for her literary reputation had this work never seen the light.

† She is said to have been much taken with the opinions of the Molinists. The spiritual repose which the author of that religious sect preached, and which then engaged the whole attention of the Inquisition, reminds us of the pleasant saying of the famous Pasquin upon this occasion :—" *If we speak, the gallies is the consequence; if we write, the gibbet; if we keep ourselves in quietness of mind, the inquisition. What then is to be done ?*"

‡ She wrote a letter to the celebrated Madame Dacier, for the purpose of exhorting her to turn catholic ; and another to a certain Count Veranau, in which she persuaded him to become a monk.

§ She is said to have been extremely fond of that vain science, notwithstanding it was one of her observations, that for judging of events, terrestrial appeared to her more sure than celestial astrology ; and that we must study astrology as we do medicine, in order to avoid becoming the dupes of either of them.

excite a sentiment of regret, in every reflecting mind, that a Queen who could think so nobly, should not have testified in her actions and conduct more desire to promote the general welfare of society.

After stating, that she fears and flatters no one, she thus proceeds:—" Are you fully persuaded of the sincerity of these new converts, the Calvinists? Men of war are strange apostles, and I think more calculated to kill, to rob, and to violate, than to persuade. I compassionate the people committed to their mercy, and I lament the ruin of so many families, and so many honest persons, who are reduced to beggary. Although in error, it seems to me, that they are more worthy of pity than of hatred. I compare France to a sick person, whose legs and arms are cut off, to cure a disease which a little patience and indulgence would have entirely healed. Nothing is more praiseworthy than the design of curing infidels and heretics, but the mode here adopted to effectuate that purpose is exceedingly strange; and as our blessed Lord has not availed himself of it to convert the world, it certainly cannot be esteemed the best." The letter is concluded by her opposing the conduct of Louis XIV. to his Protestant subjects, to that which he then held towards the Pope.

Some writers have professed to see her attachment to Protestantism in this celebrated letter ; and agreeably to this discovery they pretend, that Christina, three years afterwards, negociated with the Elector of Brandenburgh for an asylum in his dominions, in order that she might more easily carry into execution her design of returning to the Lutheran religion. If she really meditated this design, it was stopped short by the hand of nature, since she soon after that time expired.

It is pretended, that Christina died with more fortitude than Queen Elizabeth; but the contrariety* of relations respecting that event, leave it very doubtful in what manner she met her doom. Of this however there can be no dispute, that she would have obtained a higher summit of glory in the estimation of posterity, had she more imitated that illustrious personage in her steady support of Protestantism ; in her zeal, patriotizm, and skill, in government ; in her wise frugality, impartial friendship, and heroic firmness ; and in her enlightened taste for the arts and sciences.

* It is asserted by several writers, and with much appearance of truth, that her last moments were greatly disturbed by the recollection of her barbarity to Monaldeschi.

INDEX.

FINIS.

" From an attentive perusal of the volume before us, and a faithful comparison of its most prominent passages with the best sources of authority, we feel ourselves justified in saying, that Mr. Card has spared no pains, neglected no channel of information, which could qualify him for the arduous task he undertook to perform. We have not had, for many years, any history in which more useful erudition is introduced, almost uniformly illustrative of the grand questions under consideration; while the notes, which are uncommonly numerous, testify the extensive researches of the writer, and abound in matter no less curious than interesting. He has also been enabled, by judicious collation, and reference to authorities before little known, to detect the errors of preceding writers, and to expose some remarkable mistakes. But above all, the author is entitled to peculiar praise, for the manner in which he slighly notices, or skilfully compresses, circumstances that might be thought too minute and trivial for the dignity of history, and directs the attention to those important events, whether resulting from design, passion, or accident, which decide the fate of nations."—*Monthly Mirror, September*, 1805.

" The information contained in this volume is so industriously selected, so judiciously arranged, and so impartially related, that we sincerely hope Mr. Card will be prompted by the encouragement it meets with to perform his promise,—that should the public be auspicious to his present attempt, he would add the modern revolution of Catharine II. as the last link of the chain."

Monthly Magazine, Vol. XVI. No. 110.

HISTORICAL OUTLINES of the RISE and ESTABLISHMENT of the PAPAL POWER; addressed to the Roman Catholic Priests of Ireland. Octavo, 3s.

" This production, in which the rise and establishment of the papal power are traced with great ability and discrimination to the earliest sources, displays, in a most conspicious point of view, the talents of Mr. Card, who had already distinguished himself in no common way by his history of the Revolutions of Russia. It appears to have been caused by the publication of the correspondence which passed in the beginning of the present year between the Lord Chancellor of Ireland and the Earl of Fingall; and it may justly be considered as a masterly vindication of the position laid down by the former, who, speaking of addresses of a loyal tendency presented by the Roman Catholics of Ireland, says, " They are given to the winds as long as the priests of the See of Rome shall think fit to hold up to their flocks, that all who do not yield obedience to that See are guilty of rebellion against it, are not to be considered as members of the church of Christ, and, therefore, are not (in the eyes of the vulgar at least) to be considered as Christians."—*Monthly Mirror*.

" We are happy in pointing out this spirited pamphlet to the attention of our readers, who will find an important subject ably and temperately discussed, as well as much historical information communicated, with considerable vigour of style and argument."—*British Critic, July*, 1805.

" Mr. Card's work on the Rise of the Papal Power is ably written, but on the principles of high church."—*Monthly Magazine, Vol. XX. No.* 138.

[*See likewise the other periodical publications.*]

THOUGHTS upon DOMESTIC or PRIVATE EDUCATION; second edition, price 3s 6d.

" The point of controversy, whether a public or private education be preferable, which in former times was so much agitated, and has, of late years, been revived with considerable ability, is taken up by the author of the present publication with great powers of reasoning, with genuine liberality of sentiment, and in a tone of clear and impassioned eloquence, that is rarely to be found in discussions of this nature."

Monthly Mirror, May, 1807.

The REIGN of CHARLEMAGNE, considered chiefly with reference to Religion, Laws, Literature, and Manners ; in one Octavo Vol.
Price 7s. 1807.

" If, instead of dilating on the military glories of distinguished princes, the pen
of history were always employed, as Mr. Card has employed it, in recording only
their benevolent and laudable actions, how replete with instruction would be her
page; how repressed the ambition which, for the sake of being blazoned on that
page, plunges in scenes of blood that make humanity shudder. Approving his
plan, and gratified by the selection of interesting facts, presented to our consideration in this account of the reign of Charlemagne, we shall not stop to notice trivial
errors ; nor by unkind strictures, damp the ardour of abilities exerted in the sacred
cause of virtue and of science."—*British Critic.*

" The History of the Reign of this great Prince, of whom it has been truly said,
he was distinguished from the royal crowd by the prosperity of his arms, the vigour
of his government, and the reverence of distant nations, has long been a desideratum to English readers, which Mr. Card's industry and talents have at length, in
great measure, supplied."—*Oxford Review.*

" Mr. Card has succeeded in executing a work, the want of which must have
been long deplored by all who attentively examine the origin and progress of civilization. His diction is at once lively, perspicuous, and energetic ; and he frequently embellishes his subject by remarks, which evince profound judgment and a
refined taste. He has contrived to recapitulate, in a brief but clear and satisfactory
summary of 76 pages, the chief military operations and political events."

Monthly Mirror.

" Our readers will here perceive that the interior of the reign of this magnificent
monarch must contain a sufficient variety of incidents for the pursuit of his historian,
without any aberration to foreign connections. It is to such *interior department*
that the present work is chiefly devoted, and the writer has executed his task with
industry, accuracy, and elegance "—*New Annual Register for 1807.*

" This is a work which has long been a desideratum among the readers of history. " The name of Charlemagne," observes the author, who is already known to
the public by his history of the Revolutions of Russia, and other valuable performances, " is not less familiar to the learned, than to the unlearned reader : yet his
reign has been exposed to great, and 1 will venture to add, undeserved neglect :"
which defect of curiosity respecting the life and character of a man, of whose fame
the annals of Europe are full, is rightly attributed by Mr. Card to the remoteness
of the period in which Charlemagne flourished. Indeed, with the sole exception of
Gibbon, (and he has only viewed the reign of Charlemagne in such a manner as to pro-
voke, rather than satisfy our curiosity,) no other writer has manifested any desire to
render the English reader familiar with the military and political operations of that
renowned hero. To produce then a work, which, in a popular and elegant style,
should delineate Charlemagne in his public and private character, and trace the
line of policy pursued by him to impart knowledge, and to create a spirit of improvement among his people, has been attempted, and we may safely add, in most respects
performed, by Mr. Card."—*Cabinet.*

Liverpool, printed by Harris, Brothers.